Presented to

_____

by

_____

On the Occasion of

_____

Date

_____

Lessons for a
SUPER
MOM

Devotions from the Middle of Life

HELEN WIDGER
MIDDLEBROOKE

BARBOUR BOOKS
An Imprint of Barbour Publishing, Inc.

ISBN 1-58660-495-3

Cover art © Mark Matcho

All Scripture quotations are taken from the King James Version of the Bible.

All the people in this book exist or have existed. The names have been changed to protect the innocent; the names of the "guilty"—my children, husband, in-laws, deceased relatives, and Colorado mom—have not been changed but have been used with permission.

"The Romance of Girl and Boy" is an unpublished story by the late D. Bruce Widger. All rights reserved. Used by permission of the owner.

Published by Barbour Books, an imprint of Barbour Publishing, Inc., P.O. Box 719, Uhrichsville, Ohio 44683
www.barbourbooks.com

ecpa Member of the
Evangelical Christian
Publishers Association

Printed in the United States of America.
5 4 3 2 1

With thanks to Jan.

In memory of Mom.

To the Glory of God.

CONTENTS

PREFACE

I find it awkward to be writing a preface to a devotional book. The whole idea of a devotional is to help readers think about God, not about the book itself. But this book requires an explanation.

This is not your grandmother's devotional. While I aspire to write with the insight of the Puritans, Oswald Chambers, and Amy Carmichael, whose devotional writings have inspired and lifted me, I cannot.

I have not yet achieved their intimacy with the Father. My thoughts are too often down here on earth, in the trenches of life, where children laugh and fight, where tempers are lost, where prayers are prayed in desperation, not with inspiration.

But God is down here, too. God is with us where we are. And because He is here, all of life is sacred. Washing dishes is just as holy as preaching sermons.

And that's the whole point of this devotional—to help you see God in everyday life. Although we do not always sense His presence, He is there. He's not hiding, we're just not seeing.

Many of these essays first appeared in my newspaper column, "In the Middle," which was published from 1996 to 1999 in the *Aberdeen* (South Dakota) *American News*. Most of these have been edited to make sense now, although some, particularly those referring to my children at a specific age, are as they were written. I hope this will not be confusing.

These devotionals are a record of my life's journey. Many ideas are repeated. But life is like that. We humans are typically thickheaded, so we need to review God's lessons often.

Special thanks go to my husband, Mike, and my children—Matthew, John, Jane, Charles, Thomas, Anna, Benjamin, Deborah, and Audra (who arrived a year after the manuscript was finished)—for so often showing me God's hand at work, and for putting up with the writing process. Thanks also go to the readers of "In the Middle," both the newspaper column and the Internet site of the same name, who have encouraged me and prayed for me throughout this project, and to my friends Joy and Vickie who, along with Mike, proofread and edited the manuscript.

But my deepest gratitude goes to my patient Father in heaven, the Sovereign of the Universe, who has revealed Himself to me in humble ways and common circumstances. I pray this devotional will help you see Him where you are, too.

HELEN WIDGER MIDDLEBROOKE
Toto, Guam U.S.A.

SEEING GOD IN THE LIVES OF CHILDREN. . .

As a young mother, I asked the Lord to teach me of Himself and of myself through my children. He gave me eight children. Apparently, I had a lot to learn.

> *He [Elisha] took up also the mantle of*
> *Elijah that fell from him.*
> 2 KINGS 2:13

My three year old came

dashing through the dining room singing at the top of her lungs. "I've *gotta* go *pahhhty.* . . . C'mon, Mommy—I've *got to go potty.* . ."

I maneuvered between the table and high chair quickly and joined her in the bathroom. But I had been snookered—there was no crisis. She looked at me coolly.

"I can do it by myself!"

"So why did you want me?" She didn't answer, so I turned to leave.

"Don't go, Mommy."

"But you don't need me. You can do it yourself."

I left and she managed—all by herself.

"By myself!" is her favorite phrase. You name it—getting dressed, setting the table, "reading" a book—my sassy toddler insists on doing things solo.

She ran to me smiling. "TA-DA!" she sang. She pointed to her clothes. "How's dis?"

A pink-flowered top covered purple-striped shorts. The shoes were on the wrong feet. "That's good. . .ah, why are you wearing purple shorts instead of pink ones?"

"Becuz I want to."

Such independence! Where did it come from?

It could be hereditary. A certain three year old I once knew often lip-whipped adults, particularly a certain doctor she disliked. Alas, my kid's just a chip off the old block.

But why hurry so? Why must she be a "big girl" so soon?

I guess that's natural, too. When I was her age, I wanted to do everything my big brother did, do it sooner, and do it better. I wanted to grow up. But when I did, I found myself looking back, wondering why I'd been in such a hurry. And I wished for life as it used to be, safe in my mother's arms.

Of course you can't tell that to a toddler—she would not understand. Or would she?

She ran to me and wrapped her arms around my legs. *"Mommy!* Pick me up!" She hugged me then ran off to do something else.

All by herself.

. . .

My children are not my own, Father.
*You have sent them to me so I may
guide and direct them toward You.
Though I hate to let them go,
help me be faithful to pass on the mantle of faith and love
that they might serve You with wise and humble hearts.*

And the angel answering said unto him,
I am Gabriel, that stand in the presence of God;
and am sent to speak unto thee,
and to shew thee these glad tidings.
LUKE 1:19

Several years ago, Anna assumed a new identity.

"Make me an angel," she said one Saturday. She handed me a red hair band and stood perfectly still.

I put the hair band on her like a halo. It didn't look angelic, but she didn't care. She was an angel. She ran to tell her brothers.

"Hey guys! I'm an angel," she told them. Pause. *"I am so an angel! Mommy made me one!"*

Undeterred by their unbelief, she came back to me. "So where are my wings?"

"You've got to earn your wings."

She shrugged, then went flittering about the house. She flew along with me to the post office, flapping her arms. "These are my wings," she said.

Her persistence amazed me. "Hey, Angel," I said as we drove, "What are—"

She cut me off. "I not an angel anymore. I too tired. I Anna."

But her mind certainly wasn't tired. She kept thinking.

"Can angels dance?" she asked.

"Sure," I said. "On the heads of pins."

"Are angels girls? In the Christmas video, the angel's a girl."

"I don't think angels are girls. Angels are God's fighters and God's messengers. Angels look like men."

"But on the video the angel looks like a girl."

"I know. But that's not what the Bible says."

After her nap, she was back with her halo. "Make me an angel."

And so it went all weekend. Angel. Not an angel. Angel. Not an angel. Was the halo on? She was Angel. Did her mortal brothers need an unholy response? She was Anna, and she was no angel.

On Sunday, I was exhausted by the demands of mommyhood. I plopped on the couch. Anna joined me. She gave me a hug and kiss and snuggled close. "Being a mom is good," I thought. "It is a sublime thing to be loved by a little one."

Hmm. Was that a message from God?

Maybe she really was an angel after all.

. . .

Father, thank You for the messages
You send through my children.
Help me hear Your mighty voice in their innocent words
and feel Your compassion through their loving actions.

For what is your life?
It is even a vapour,
that appeareth for a little time,
and then vanisheth away.
JAMES 4:14

February 1997

My firstborn, Matthew, is thirteen, and I am full of wonder.

I wonder how he got to be so old so fast. Thirteen already!? It seems just a breath ago I first whispered his name.

I wonder where the baby went. Where's the tooth-less smile, the innocent giggle, the hands that barely grasped a rattle? Now a young man strides through my house, looking very mature with a baby brother on his shoulder.

Where's the toddler who had a million questions, who sought me out when he needed wisdom? He's now a budding scientist with his own answers.

Somewhere between the booties and the Nikes, I must have fallen asleep. Or maybe I just wasn't watching closely enough. Sure, I saw changes—a lost tooth here, an outgrown shoe there—but in the busyness of life, I sometimes overlooked the bigger picture; he was a boy headed toward manhood.

Suddenly, he's thirteen and at the threshold. And I wonder: Is he prepared? Have I given him the tools

17

he needs to forge his own life? Will he be equipped before he goes through the door in another five or six short years?

More than anything, I wonder how he's become so much older, while I've hardly aged at all. Why, aside from a few wrinkles, I look the same as I did the day he was born. (Okay, okay! Almost the same.)

Plus I've become wiser.

And so has he.

One morning he blindsided me.

"Mom! Your hair!"

I turned and looked at him, eye to eye. "What about it?"

"It's got gray in it!"

"It's been there awhile. You just didn't see it."

"But there's a lot of it! Especially on the side!"

"It comes with age. Like zits."

"Guys! Mom's got gray hair!"

I smiled and bit my tongue.

Yeah, he's thirteen all right.

Only five more years to go.

. . .

Dear Father, these blessings You give are so fleeting.
Before I know it, they are grown and gone.
Slow me down and open my eyes,
so I may treasure the precious time I have with my children.

For in many things we offend all.
JAMES 3:2

I should have said no.

There wasn't time for a haircut—he had to catch the camp bus in thirty minutes. Besides, for two years he had said buzz cuts look stupid.

But I said yes. So he sat down on the kitchen stool amid the rising tide of siblings.

I went to work with the clippers: Up the back, up the sides. Step over the baby.

I stopped. "You're sure you want it all buzzed?"

"I'm sure."

Back to work: Off the top with the thick, red hair. Step around the baby. Move the preschooler. One more stroke and—

OOPS!

The guide came off the clippers! In a split second I had made a hole in his haircut! He had been fuzzed, not buzzed!

"Get me a wig! I can't go to camp like this!"

Wailing, I left the room to let his father deal with the problem.

When the tears subsided, we sent him to camp under a ball cap, which would stay on all week. But after one hot afternoon, he decided to get fuzzed all over. I got him a cooler Aussie-style bush hat. He felt a little better.

But I still felt guilty. I had ruined my ten year old's life for camp week. I made a mistake, but he paid for it. Would he ever forgive me? Would he be forever maladjusted for having spent the summer looking like a grunt? What had I done?

Mother-guilt is very inhibiting. And there's so much of it around today. Thanks to the experts, we modern moms think our every action will mar our kids for life.

Yes, we can make serious, life-changing errors. But most mistakes are not forever. Kids are more resilient than we think.

I know, because my mom once made a mistake. She accidentally gave me aspirin and almost killed me. But I survived the allergic reaction, and I forgave her.

Some day after summer's end, my son will forgive me.

Then he'll find a new barber.

. . .

I am not perfect, Father;
sometimes I fail, sometimes I offend.
Sometimes those offenses hurt my children.
Help me be humble before my little ones
that I may restore their confidence in me.
And let us all find grace to help in time of need.

Before destruction the heart of man is haughty,
and before honour is humility.
PROVERBS 18:12

I should have said no—again.

It wasn't the time for a haircut. It was after 10 P.M.—
it was time for bed. Especially for a tired mother who
had been operating all day on four hours' sleep. But
he begged.

"I'm tired," I said. "I don't feel like cutting hair."
He begged more.

"I need to go to bed." He got out the clippers,
scissors, and drape.

"I didn't say I was going to do it." He sat down.

"You remember camp two years ago?"

Yes, he remembered the day the clipper guide broke
in the middle of a buzz cut. He went to camp with a
new hat, which hid a very prominent patch of fuzz.

Yet he continued pleading. He had to have a buzz
cut. His hair was too long, too hot. Clearly, he was
desperate. And I was too tired to fight.

So it was that I plugged in the clippers, secured
the broken guide with my finger, and began shearing
his thick red mop.

Buzzzzz. Up the back. *Buzzzzz.* Up the left side.
Buzzzzz. Up the right side.

All that was left was a Mohawk-like strip on top.
"I think I'll stop there. See what you think."

He thought it was kind of "cool" and threatened to keep it. But he came back to have the job finished.

BUZ—the clippers caught a knot! My finger slipped! The guide came off. And—

"Noo!!! I did it again!!!"

On top of his head was a near-bald patch. I dropped the clippers and began to cry. He ran to a mirror and, to my amazement, laughed.

When the emotions subsided, I turned the buzz cut into a fuzz cut. I wanted to say, "You should have learned from history." Instead, I just apologized over and over.

"It's okay, Mom," he reassured me. "I shouldn't have pushed you to do it when you were tired. It looks okay."

It certainly does.

Especially beneath his new hat.

. . .

My children do not always learn from history,
and neither do I.
Let me not be so proud as to think that
anything I do is new or grand,
for there is nothing new under the sun.
Let me not think that I can do anything without You.
And those times that I fall,
let me know You are always the same,
always loving and forgiving,
and ever willing to give me another chance.

And, ye fathers,
provoke not your children to wrath:
but bring them up in the nurture
and admonition of the Lord.

<small>EPHESIANS 6:4</small>

My, how time flies!

The baby is already a year old!

I love the first year—the growth, the spontaneity, the discovery. For a baby, every day is an adventure. There's always something new to do or see or feel.

It's amazing what has happened in 365 short days. He's gone from being a serene armful to being an active handful; from crying to communicating; from sweet to stubborn.

And it's amazing how much I've done in those days. I've been his major food source. I've changed more than eleven hundred diapers. I've done extra laundry every week, and I've given him all but one of his baths.

I've walked the floor with him, taken him for checkups, worried about his development, hauled him to therapy. I've taken pictures and given hugs (not enough of either). I've rocked him until I've fallen to sleep exhausted.

Also amazing, in its own peculiar way, is how little child care the dad in this house has done in that time. He has slept through night feedings, changed a handful of diapers, held him only until he cried.

But that's an observation, not a complaint. Most dads—including the one in this house—work outside the home. They earn the money that enables children to thrive, which is just as important as changing diapers and walking floors.

That's not to absolve dads from all child care—babies need a father's touch as much as a mother's—it's just a recognition that distinct male and female roles are important to a child's development.

Sure, I wouldn't mind more help with baby maintenance, but I'll manage.

Besides, I do get a few rewards. While Dad's out working, I get to watch the baby grow. I get to see the first smile, cheer the first step, hear the first words.

And after waiting for months, the first words finally came: "Da-Da! Da-Da! Da!"

What?! After all I've given, he dares to say "Da-Da"? Now *that's* amazing.

. . .

Although I sometimes think I'm
the only person in my babies' lives,
help me remember that I'm only one of many given
to them to make them the persons You want them to be.
I'm grateful for all the souls
who will bless them along the way.
And please give my husband wisdom and patience to do his
part to nurture them in the Lord.

Thine eyes did see my substance,
yet being unperfect;
and in thy book all my members were written.
PSALM 139:16

Where do kids come from?

I'm not talking physically. Forget the egg, sperm, and zygote stuff. I'm talking personality. Where do some kids come from?

Baby Ben, for example, likes to draw on unusual surfaces. He uses crayons, markers, pencils, pens. . . He scribbles on walls, file cabinets, air filters, windowsills, wallpaper. . .

Some toddlers do this, I know. But not *my* toddlers. I've never had one who regularly wrote on walls. But now here's Ben (and his crayon). Where did he come from?

Then there's my Jane. She is truly artistic. At age three, she drew caricatures—people with large heads and small bodies. Now she can draw almost anything she sees, and she's especially good with cartoons.

This amazes me. My artistic creations are limited to blocks of type, photos, and lines, for which I need a ruler. Where did I get a kid with such talent?

And consider Charles, who does multi-digit calculations in his head, transposes music, and remembers every joke he's ever read. But he can't tie his shoes. Where did he come from?

It's not really a difficult question.

Each child is a unique creation of a loving God, who calls genetic material together to make the individual as He desires. He has deemed that a child is not a sum, but a product, of the parents' genetic makeup. It's really no wonder if a kid is different from his parents.

Some children, though, are very much the same.

I thought of this the dark morning after Thanksgiving, while standing in line with John, The Persistent One, waiting for a store to open.

"Why am I doing this again?" I said.

"I bet down deep you're thinking, 'It sure would be nice to win a hundred dollars,' " he said.

I shook my head.

He reconsidered: "I bet down real deep you're thinking, 'I wonder where I got a kid like this?' "

Wrong again. With this kid, I never wonder.

He looks like his dad. He acts like his mom. He has many of my childhood qualities, good and bad, only more so. I've never questioned his roots.

With him, my concern is not where he's come from, but where he's going and how he'll get there.

We gave him good roots. But can we give him strong wings?

I wonder.

Father, help me love my children
as You have made them.
Remind me daily that each one is
a precious gift from You and each has been
created for a special task in Your kingdom.
Please give me wisdom to direct them to that task.

And God made two great lights;
the greater light to rule the day,
and the lesser light to rule the night:
he made the stars also.

GENESIS 1:16

The silence is broken!

Benjamin is talking!

It took two years for him to speak for himself. And now that he can talk, he won't shut up.

And now that he can talk, I'm wondering why I ever wished he would.

Just kidding. I enjoy this stage of life. Benjamin is so excited about everything he sees and learns. I just get a little weary of hearing about his discoveries again and again and again.

Since he's found the moon, for example, a night is not complete without at least one sighting.

"Mamamama!" he'll shout. He'll drag me to a window and point: "Moooon!"

Before we can resume life, we'll have to check for the moooon at every window.

"Mama, moooon?! Mama, *moooon?"*

"Moon's gone," I'll say. "Let's look for stars."

"TARS! Tars, Mommy. Tars!"

When he tires of that, he'll go back to the moon window. "Mooon, Mommy, Moon!"

Withstanding his developing communication skills

take lots of patience on my part. But that's not enough. I also need creativity and a new dictionary because Ben's "yes" is "yayz," but his "no" may be "(s)no(w)."

"Bennese" is amazingly compact and necessarily contextual. I have to really pay attention.

If it's 8:30 A.M., "oh" usually means "(t)oh(st)." But if he's in the tub, "oh" means "(b)oh(t)." And if he has bare feet, "oh" is his big "(t)oh."

Ben has a "dahhddy" (the funny guy who chases him around the house) and a "daaggy" (the four-legged critter that steals his blankie). But when he points to the dish on the floor and says, "dahgdy's oood," I picture Mike eating Dog Chow.

Food words are important to Ben. He likes "peeezz," "(j)uerce" (juice), "days" (dates), "ammole" (apple), and "aregeh" (orange). If he really wants to butter me up, he'll say, "(p)weezzzzz, Mommy!"

Although I'm almost fluent in Bennese, some-times the kid spouts a string of authentic frontier gib-berish that leaves me dazed. Then I just smile, nod, and wait for the day when he's totally understandable.

That day will come too soon.

Before I'm ready, he'll be saying that I don't know anything; that he wants to borrow the car; that he loves another woman.

Then I'll long for the day when happiness was in the moooon.

And joy was in the 'tars.

Father, You have shown me the wonders of
creation through the eyes of a toddler.
Your creation is truly marvelous;
the works of Your hands, a joy to behold.
I praise You for the gift of language,
that allows us to share our joys with others.

Let your speech be alway with grace,
seasoned with salt,
that ye may know how
ye ought to answer every man.
COLOSSIANS 4:6

I had the distinct impression
I was being followed.

I turned to find myself thigh-to-eye with my preschooler.

"Mom, can I have my car?"

"Where is it?"

"In the attic, by the boxes."

"If you know where it is, you may get it."

"I can't."

I went to the attic with him. He showed me the car, which was behind boxes in a crawl space near the open stairwell.

"See, I can't get it," he said emphatically. "I'd break my neck!"

"You might have," I said, handing him the car. "Good thinking."

As we went down the steps I had to smile. It was not the first time I had heard myself coming out of his mouth, but it was the most gratifying. He had finally learned that some actions are dangerous.

Other times, my little mirror is not as gracious. He reflects me at less than my best. One day he and his little sister were sitting on the couch with books in their laps. "We're having Quiet Time," he announced. His bigger siblings in the adjoining room ignored him, talking loudly over a blaring radio.

"Hey guys, shut up!" he bellowed. *"We're having quiet time!"*

Ouch! The irony was cutting. Surely I don't sound that bad in the morning, do I? To him I must.

Hearing my words fall from my children's lips can be humbling, but it also gives me hope: I am getting through to them. My expressions and beliefs are taking root in their hearts; the family identity is taking hold. They are sharing in the verbal and spiritual heritage I drew from my mother, who drew from her mother, who drew from her mother (all the way back to Eve, who saw Cain in a tree and yelled, "Get down from there! You'll break your neck!").

Some day, their children will talk like they talk. It will be sweet revenge.

I hope I live to hear it.

. . .

Father, guard my tongue this day.
Keep my temper even, my words sweet, my spirit calm.
Let my children hear as well as see Jesus in me.

And he is before all things,
and by him all things consist.
COLOSSIANS 1:17

I sat on the couch talking with a friend, watching my firstborn.

A little over a year old, he was so cute, so sweet. A cause of surprise, not suspicion.

"You've got to watch boys," Bess warned. "They can take apart anything."

She spoke from experience. Her preschool boy had already disassembled several things that no one could put back together.

I didn't doubt her words at all. I had already been warned.

At ten months of age, Matthew had deftly opened a milk jug with a twist-on cap. That's when I began to worry.

"Your motor coordination is not supposed to be that good yet," I told him. "Don't you read the books?"

He smiled at me as if to say, "Just wait, Mom. You ain't seen nothin' yet."

Before he was two, he could open baby powder cans and Desitin tubes and distribute the contents in minutes. He broke a pedal on a piano that had withstood moves to Guam and back. He could empty a cupboard in seconds.

Then we added a second boy!

And nothing stayed together after that.

Between them, they could undo a clean room in five seconds, washed faces in two seconds, and freshly made beds instantly. As they got bigger, they dissected toys, radios, bicycles, a computer, and a mimeograph.

They—and their siblings (especially the boys)—are the Second Law of Thermodynamics come to life. (This law states that in any spontaneous change, the entropy—or randomness—of the universe increases.)

When they undo something, it stays undone. In the rare times that they add energy to a closed system, such as their bedroom, the resulting order is temporary.

Ordinarily, their uncanny ability to undo things gives them more trouble than it's worth. They sometimes miss fun opportunities because they need to put things back together.

But once their entropic impulses were rewarded.

A friend wanted The Destructive Duo to remove an entire deck—for pay. They took the job eagerly, estimating they could destroy it in three hours.

With crowbars and screwdrivers in hand, they systematically dismantled her husband's craftsmanship. Although slowed by "tons" of screws, they had the deck off in less than six hours.

"The neighbors didn't think those two little boys could get the deck off in a week, let alone a day," my friend reported.

Oh, if they only knew!

They ain't seen nothin' yet.

. . .

*Lord, I'm so grateful that You
can and do hold my world together,
even when my children take it apart.
In Your hand I can rest securely.*

I have called upon thee,
for thou wilt hear me, O God:
incline thine ear unto me, and hear my speech.
PSALM 17:6

One of my heart's deepest desires is to truly communicate with my children.

I want to know them; I want them to know me.

But that's easier said than done. And it's getting harder as the years go by.

At first I thought talking with a two year old was tough. But the truth is, it's really very simple. The first rule in talking with two year olds is that you can't talk with two year olds. You talk *at* and *to* them; rarely with them.

To survive the twos all you need are patience, humor, and ten phrases: Yes. No. I love you. Because I said so. Go potty. Pick up your toys. Be nice. Don't touch. Get your finger out of your nose. It's bedtime.

By age three, my children usually can converse. But to understand them, I must be a master of toddler trivia. I must know, for example, my three year old's sound substitutions. "Benzahmen's fweeping" means the baby is not awake. And when she says, "The eagle woke me up," I must know her big brother likes to pretend he's an eagle.

The optimum age for understanding is between five and nine. They know how to speak, their vocabularies are better, and they still believe me. It's a wonderful time. I talk, they listen, and vice versa.

After the tenth birthday, they develop selective deafness. I talk, but they don't hear me. (Unless I'm in the closet, talking long distance to Grandma about presents.) This condition worsens until adolescence when they become selectively dumb. I talk; they hear—sometimes; they respond—sometimes. . .maybe. . .if they feel like it.

The other day, my thirteen-year-old city boy looked as though he had been farming.

"You need a bath," I said.

He stared at me as if I were from Mars. Slowly, his lip began to quiver. And then—he talked!

"Awwww, Mom."

My heart began to flutter.

At last! We had communicated!

. . .

*Even though I can't always
communicate with those around me,
I can communicate with You anytime, Father.
Forgive me for not always availing myself
of Your ever present ear.
Let me learn to pray without ceasing
and to listen to You without interrupting.*

To him the porter openeth; and the sheep hear his voice:
and he calleth his own sheep by name,
and leadeth them out.

JOHN 10:3

My children are suffering from an identity crisis.

Not that it's their fault; they know who they are.

The problem is, I don't.

On any given day, I will call at least one of them by the wrong name.

Sometimes, I'll go through the whole roster before I get it right. (I sound like Snow White calling the dwarves for supper.) "Matthew-no-John-no-Tom. . . ah, Charles. . .oh, whoever you are—get over here."

It gets ridiculous. Once one of them called me to see his headstand. I saw only his feet and an upside down face. And the first words from my mouth were: "Very good, ah, which kid are you?"

"Charles," he said disgustedly.

"Yes, I guess you are," I muttered.

He was miffed, and I was frustrated. I named these children, for goodness' sake! I ought to be able to get their names right the first time, every time. Yet I don't.

And I've never met a mother who did. My own mother called the roster regularly, and there were only three of us.

I can't explain it. I think something happens during

the second pregnancy. Maybe too many hormones mess up the connection between the eyes and the mouth. Or maybe it's just a Mother Thing.

The Kid Thing is to roll the eyes and put up with it, which most of my children do.

But then there's the sassy three year old. She has started fighting fire with fire. She changes her own name several times a day, depending on her favorite fantasy.

"Anna!" I'll call.

"I not Anna," she'll say, "I Cindurwelwa." She'll twirl and dance pretending to be at a ball. This will last until I use the new name: "Cinderella!"

"I not Cindurwelwa," she'll say, showing me her doll. "I Mairwy. This is Jesus."

The next time I'll try "Mary-Cinderella."

But she'll look at me with an impish grin and say, "I still Anna."

And I'm still Mommy. . .I think.

. . .

Father, how I rejoice that even though
I am one of millions of the chosen, You know my name.
You never "call the roster" when I call upon You.
How it humbles me to think that
You not only know my name, but also my thoughts,
my dreams, my joys, and sorrows. You know me!
Let me someday realize my desire to know You
as intimately as I am known.

That this may be a sign among you,
that when your children ask their fathers
in time to come, saying,
What mean ye by these stones?
Then ye shall answer them. . .
these stones shall be for a memorial
unto the children of Israel for ever.
JOSHUA 4:6–7

The sassy one turned four in 1998.

In the weeks before her birthday, I spent many hours making an album for her. About time. Her pictures had been piling up since birth. The last time I updated albums I was expecting her.

I got one of those photo-safe, acid-free, lignin-free, scrapbook-type albums, designed to last her lifetime and longer. Then I went to work.

Before I could sort pictures, I had to find pictures. That was the hardest part.

Pulling her photos out of the family picture pool was easy—she was the blond baby in pink—but organizing them was another matter. Which Christmas was this? What year was that? Was she two or three then? Where's the first step, the second birthday?

At first, I was overwhelmed.

As I arranged, cropped, rearranged, and mounted photos, my feelings changed. This was not just a gift. This was her life, from the birthing room in Maine to the living room in South Dakota. And I had the thrill of watching it all unfold again.

I soon realized how much the album mattered. The toy I'd give her might not last the summer and she'd outgrow the dress. But she'd never outgrow the scrapbook; she might even pass it on to another generation.

Perhaps that sense of permanence is why "scrapbooking" is one of the fastest growing crafts in the country. Preserving things that have been is just as important as giving children new things. A sense of history strengthens the hope for the future.

But there is a drawback—scrapbooks don't stay updated long. Kids keep growing and changing and making memories to capture.

"I'm gonna have another burstday and then I'll be five," she announced.

Sigh. The hurrier she goes, the behinder I get.

It's a wonderful futility.

. . .

*Lord, those who have gone before me have left
so many precious pictures, clipping, and reminders.
Let me make new memories and memorials,
so my children know who they are and Whose they are.
Let them go into the future with a sense of the past.*

Thou hast given him his heart's desire,
and hast not withholden the request of his lips.
PSALM 21:2

For the first two years of his life, Ben rarely uttered a syllable.

At first, this didn't concern me because each child has waited longer to talk. Either they don't need to talk (Ben's sisters talked for him), or they just can't get a word in edgewise.

But by his second birthday, I was starting to worry. With visions of trips to the speech therapist and of his being branded "developmentally delayed," I began wishing he would speak.

My wish came true.

Sometime between two and three, the floodgate opened and the words started spilling out. Then, perhaps in an effort to make up for lost time, Ben talked. And talked. And talked.

For one so small, his grammar was quite good— he was adept at using pronouns—but his pronunciations needed work. He regularly substituted T for K, Y for L, and F for CR. Ordinarily, he was easy to understand. But when he got excited, conversations got tedious.

One night he was very excited. He came running into my bedroom with a handful of Duplo blocks.

"Mommy! See I made!"

"What is it?"

"I dunno. Make somet'ing else." He sat on the bed and pulled the blocks apart. "Make somet'ing for you."

"Are you going to make me a house?"

"No, make a puter."

"A pluter?"

"No. P'ter."

"What's a peter?"

"Not peter, puter." He shook his head. How stupid can a mother get?

"OH! Puter! You're making me a computer?"

"Yeah, Mommy."

"But you can't make a computer."

He paused, looked at his blocks, and smiled. "Make house."

We played with the blocks more. He told me when to add a block and where to put it. Then he decided to charm me out of my hard-earned cash.

"Want penny. P'ease Mommy—have penny?"

"Why do you want a penny?"

"I wike pennies."

"I like them, too. What would you do with it if I gave it to you?"

"Put in your dwoor."

"If you're going to put it in my drawer, why should I give it to you in the first place?"

"Betuz."

And on it went. Until my ears were ready to fall off.

To think I wished for this!
After so many, you'd think I'd have known better.

. . .

Forgive me for getting weary of my blessings, Lord.
Thank You for giving me my desire,
to have my baby talk.
Let me teach him to guard his tongue
and to use it to build up those around him.

O clap your hands, all ye people;
shout unto God with the voice of triumph.
PSALM 47:1

My mother was a schoolteacher, and she knew children very well.

Over the years, she formulated several indisputable truths about children.

Truth Number One: Third children are always the loudest and friendliest.

The axiom held true in the three-kid families we knew. In our house, the third one had the loudest mouth and was the most outgoing.

When I became a mother, I expected the axiom would hold. I wasn't disappointed. Number three was the first girl, Jane. And she had the loudest, shrillest baby scream I had ever heard. That scream once drove a nurse practitioner out of an exam room.

As more children came, I wondered what would happen. Was it possible each new one would be louder than the last?

Numbers four and five are only slightly louder than number three, who has become quieter with age. But number six, Anna, has proven her grandmother's thesis, at least twice over.

You'd never know it to look at her. Anna looks quiet. She's petite, with golden-brown hair and a sweet face. Put her in a blue dress and you'd think she fell off a Renoir painting.

But when she opens her mouth, cover your ears!

She talks LIKE THIS. ALMOST ALL THE TIME!

You can hear her throughout the house. She can out-shout all of her siblings combined.

This can be useful. If I need to wake someone, Anna can rouse the dead. And if I need to holler for someone, she saves my vocal cords.

But toning her down is difficult. A "meek and quiet spirit" she's not. One day while I was attempting to rest, she was PLAYING AND TALKING WITH HER FAVORITE BROTHER. She kept coming to ask me QUESTIONS, but eventually left when I said I didn't want to be disturbed.

She went down the hall to PLAY QUIETLY.

I was nearly asleep when she went down the hall and let out a CRY. Shocked into wakefulness, I hollered. "Anna!"

"WHAT?" she said running to my door. "I DIDN'T DISTURB YOU."

"You were making noise in the hall."

"I'M SORRY." And so it goes.

I wonder what is to come.

Number seven was silent for awhile, but he's getting louder each day.

And now I'm pregnant with number eight.

At birth, this one will probably let out the "shout

heard round the world."

When I'm buying diapers, I'd better buy ear plugs.

. . .

Lord, let my praises of You be
as loud and happy as my children's voices.
Let me not be afraid to make a joyful noise,
for You alone are worthy of my greatest praise.

Keep thy heart with all diligence;
for out of it are the issues of life.
PROVERBS 4:23

One night I took my daughters along to a baby shower.

We indulged in shower goodies and stayed out beyond their bedtime.

On the way home, Jane fell asleep in the backseat. But Anna was on overdrive from all the goodies. She bubbled all the way home.

Her mouth was wired straight to her brain; every thought was articulated. I was her captive audience— I had to listen, even though I didn't want to.

The flood began after we filled our water jugs and were headed home. I had pulled out of the parking lot without turning on my lights.

Within a minute, a patrolman was driving along side of us, shouting.

"Ma'am! Your lights!"

I turned on the lights and thanked him.

"Mommy," Anna said as she watched him drive away, "what was the powiceman's name?"

"I don't know. Mr. Policeman, I suppose."

"Where does he live?"

"I don't know."

There were other questions I don't remember, but within minutes, she had forgotten Mr. Policeman and was engaged in a concert of songs from Sunday school.

"Jesus loves the little children. . . ."

"Mr. Bo is our Sunday school teacher," she said in a song break. "His wife helps him, but we can't say the rest of their name, so we just call them Mr. Bo and Mrs. Bo."

She paused.

"I like them," she declared. "They like me."

"That's because you're such a nice girl," I said.

The comment didn't seem to register. She went back to singing.

"Mommy, you sing. . ."

"But I don't know that song. You need to teach it to me."

She tried, but was making up the words and couldn't do it the same twice. She gave it up and went on to another song and another story.

The miles clicked off as her tongue clicked on. Soon we were on the last leg of the trip, going up a steep hill. Though late, there were other cars on the road.

"There's a car in front of us and a car behind us," she observed. "Who's driving that car?"

"I don't know."

"Where do they live?"

"Anna, I don't know the person; how can I possibly know where they live?"

By the time we got home, I felt really stupid. I had not been able to answer any of my five year old's questions.

But I did know what was important to Anna. She cares about other people, what their names are, where they live. She's happy knowing that people and Jesus love her. And she's not afraid to sing.

I also knew I had been given a precious look inside a tender heart.

I'm so glad I had to listen.

· · ·

Father, You have shown me the tender heart of a child,
and reminded me of what is most important—
that we love and are loved, that we care about others.
Let my little one keep her heart tender
and please let me recover the tenderness
I've lost through stress and busyness.
Let me never forget that all life and lives are precious.

Know ye not that they which
run in a race run all,
but one receiveth the prize?
So run, that ye may obtain.

1 CORINTHIANS 9:24

To my surprise,
I've become the mother of a card shark!

Three-year-old Ben has developed an affinity for cards. Not evil poker cards, but colorful, fun, kid cards like Uno and Garfield Crazy Eights.

I've never had a toddler so interested in cards. After watching his siblings playing Uno (kid's version), he wanted to play, too. For his recent birthday all he wanted was "Uno tards."

He got his wish, much to my chagrin. Then a few weeks after his birthday, we all got the flu. We played more games of Uno than I cared to count. And no matter how many games we played, he always had to play one more.

And now almost every morning I'm greeted by a sweet, smiling face that has one request: "P'ay Uno wit' me?"

Playing Uno with Ben is an adventure. You're never sure what's going to happen or how things are going to proceed. The only thing certain is that he's going to "win."

A typical game goes like this:

Because he's too little, I "shovel" (shuffle) the cards.

Then he deals. Maybe five cards, maybe more. Sometimes he deals from the top, sometimes not. Sometimes he gets more than I, or vice versa. He stops when he thinks he's done.

He turns over the top card to form the discard pile, and puts down the draw pile.

"I go first," he'll say. Then he'll play any card he wants. I try to encourage him to match color or number, but he doesn't always agree.

To be a good example, I always play a correct card, in the hope he'll eventually reciprocate.

But he rarely does. He plays whatever he wants. If I go out first, he'll continue putting down cards until he happily "wins."

And then we do it over again. And again. And again.

I keep playing because Ben's style intrigues me. I like to watch how he reasons. Even if I lose, I still win because I've spent time with him.

Besides, I like analogies, and playing cards with Ben is like life. You never know how it's going to go. And if you play by the rules, you can bet the guy who doesn't is going to "win."

But if you do lose playing honestly, you will win because you've spent your life wisely.

One of these days, Ben will play according to the rules, and it will be so nice and predictable.

I hope it's not too soon.

Father, in this unpredictable world,
I am glad I can be sure of You.
And I can be sure that if I remain faithful
to my calling in Christ and
walk in a manner worthy of that calling,
even if I come in last, I'll be a winner.

And Jesus increased in wisdom and stature,
and in favour with God and man.
LUKE 2:52

On February 2, 2000, my firstborn turned sixteen.

Sixteen!

For Matthew, it was a milestone. Now he could get a driver's license. That alone told him that he is growing up.

For me, it was a day of memories.

I remembered the perfect little round face I beheld in that operating room. How could it now be oblong, and in need of a shave?

I could cuddle his shoulders in the crook of my arm then. How could they be so broad that I need two arms to encircle them?

How did the sweet soprano gurgle grow into a baritone groan?

The little boy I looked down to in tender love, I now must look up at, sometimes with tough love.

The little legs that once struggled to stand are now muscular, strong, and fast.

How did he get so big so fast?

How did I miss it?

Did it slip by me as I was tending to each new baby? While I was marveling at their precious little lives, did I miss the miracle of growth that was happening in their biggest brother?

While I was muttering about the clothes he left on the floor, was I mindful that the shirts and pants were getting larger?

When I told him to stop his endless chattering, did I really notice that both the voice and the subject matter had become deeper?

Gradually but suddenly he's sixteen. No longer a baby. Not even a boy. Rather he's a young man, who in a moment's time will be out of my door and on his own.

Will he know what to do when he faces the world alone? Will he have the knowledge, the courage, the humor it takes to make it? Will he have the good sense to trust in God, knowing that with God all things are possible?

Will he be ready? Probably. Probably more ready than I'll be.

. . .

I think he's mine, Lord,
but I know my firstborn is really Yours.
As I gave him to You at birth, so I entrust him to You now.
Give him eyes to see where You are leading;
strengthen his feet so he can follow without stumbling.

But without faith
it is impossible to please him:
for he that cometh to God must believe that he is,
and that he is a rewarder of them
that diligently seek him.

HEBREWS 11:6

My sixteen year old has started to think!

His thinker is going so much now that he's almost thought himself crazy. If his thoughts don't soon undo him, they certainly will undo me.

No moment is safe. When I least expect it, Matthew will ambush me, unloading his arsenal of Difficult Questions.

"How do you really pray?"

"How can I be sure I'm saved?"

"If I don't want to go to heaven right now, does that mean I'm not saved?

"How do you really love God?"

"If I'm saved, why don't I feel like it?"

Often, I cannot answer his questions right. That is, I'll often give him answers, but they are not the ones he wants. I give him principles to apply over time; he wants easy directions to follow—NOW! He wants to be an "instant" Christian, one who is totally mature without having to put in the work.

He's been struggling with the genuineness of his own faith. He's not sure if the beliefs he has are really his, or if he has just accepted our beliefs without thinking.

"That's the problem with growing up in a Christian home," he said. "When you're saved, there's no difference. If you were saved out of a bad home, at least you'd see a difference."

He's right. Children who grow up in homes where Christ is named do have a certain spiritual disadvantage. They are so accustomed to Christian ideas and biblical teaching that they tend to believe by osmosis. Rather than getting their faith firsthand, they take it by hearsay. Though they may be genuinely saved, they often fail when tested because they only have the "faith of their fathers," not faith of their own.

His words cut me to the heart. I've fallen short of challenging my children in their growth. Instead of guiding them to seek God on their own, I've been content to create a reasonably "Christian" atmosphere, which insulates them from the world, but does not push them to know Him.

Thankfully, something from within is pushing Matthew. He's making plans to go to a Christian college and he wants to be sure of himself.

"I don't want to be a fake. I need to know now."

He may not be able to know now, but he will know someday. God will reward Matthew, because he is seeking.

And thinking.

*Father, forgive me for being
content to protect my children
from the world without pushing them toward You.
Give me the discernment I need
to answer the tough questions,
but not the toughest ones.
Teach me to shut my mouth
so they can hear You better.*

But that no man is justified
by the law in the sight of God,
it is evident: for,
The just shall live by faith.
GALATIANS 3:11

One morning, I was quietly sitting in my office when my son burst in.

One look and I knew a Difficult Question was coming.

"I didn't finish my quiet time," he said. "Is it okay to pray while I walk the dog?"

Whew! At last, an easy one.

"Paul said, 'pray without ceasing,' " I said. "It's okay to pray while you walk the dog. And the way your dog walks, it's highly advisable."

He left relieved.

But I was still concerned. Had I given him the best answer? Yes, I had answered the obvious question. But I overlooked the real issue, which was: "Will God acknowledge my prayer even if I don't pray it during devotions?"

My son, bless his heart, is struggling with his understanding of God, who He is, what He is like. Because God is too big for him to grasp, he tends to look at and respond to just one part of Him at a time.

For example, if the Bible says we should "rise up early" to pray, then he's going to rise up early and pray. And if he fails to get up early, or falls asleep during prayer, then he thinks he has failed God and God will "get him" for it.

But God is not like that. God is not a legalist.

God is a loving, infinite, patient God. He is not a divine scorekeeper. He's not sitting in heaven with a tally sheet watching how well we fill in the blanks of the Christian life. One reason He gave us the law was to show us that we could not keep it on our own, that we needed a Savior.

God is not some cosmic killjoy who is just waiting for us to mess up so He can give us "what we deserve." We all deserve an eternity in hell, but He sent His Son to save us from that. Now that we are His, will He pour out His wrath on us? Never!

Certainly, God wants obedience, but it's an obedience of a cheerful heart happily following where the Father leads, not a dutiful obedience to a set of rigid rules and regulations.

I pray someday my son will understand this.

It will make all of his Difficult Questions easier.

. . .

Father, help us all to see You as You are.
Yes, You are divine and holy,
but You look upon Your children in tenderness and love.
Each day You give us new mercies to make it through
this sin-cursed world, and I am grateful.
Help us to learn of You and so find rest for our souls.

I will praise thee;
for I am fearfully and wonderfully made:
marvelous are thy works;
and that my soul knoweth right well.
PSALM 139:14

I never cease to be amazed at the things my children can do.

This wonderment started when Matthew was a baby. At two weeks old, he smiled. At three weeks, he giggled! Both times, I was stunned. "You're too little to do that," I'd say. And he just kept on smiling.

At ten months, he unscrewed the cap on a milk jug. "You're not reading the baby books," I'd say. "You're not supposed to do that yet."

Being the precocious firstborn, he did almost everything early.

But not to be outdone, his siblings have found their own ways to amaze me.

John said his first word at ten months, then promptly shut up for another two years.

Jane picked up a pencil at age three and started drawing cartoons. Her drawings are quite humorous. One of these days, she'll be drawing comic strips.

Charles amazes me with his mathematical ability. He started counting at age three. By age four, he could count by twos—even or odd numbers—beyond one hundred. Now ten, he does long division in his head faster than on paper.

Thomas continues to mystify me with his Lego expertise. He can look at almost anything and build it out of little plastic blocks.

Anna has a level of compassion beyond her years. If I'm in a bad mood, I can count on her to bring me out of it. Somehow, she always knows what to say to lift a hurting soul.

And Ben is a budding computer hack. When he was two, I left my office with an untitled document on the screen. He shut down the computer after first saving the file!

Watching my children grow up has been one delightful astonishment after another. Each new discovery reminds me of the wonderful potential of every human being, and fills me with awe for the God who made us.

But there is a flip side to the wonder.

One night while simply walking to the van after church, Charles fell over his feet and broke his leg!

Just how did he do that?

Sometimes life is just too amazing.

. . .

Father, *when I consider my children,*
these works of Your hands, I am truly amazed.
And when I think that You have used me
as Your creative vessel, I am humbled.
I am grateful You count me worthy to lead Your little ones.

The soul of the sluggard desireth, and hath nothing:
but the soul of the diligent shall be made fat.
PROVERBS 13:4

It's been twenty years since I met Eddie.

Eddie was a skinny junior-higher back then, the son of my first boss. And he was every teacher's nightmare: short attention span, hyperactive, spontaneous; smart, but unmotivated.

A real drive-you-nuts kind of kid, he was an interruption on two feet.

Eddie and I became buddies when he had leg surgery. He had to wear a full-leg cast for many weeks and couldn't go to school. I was his tutor.

Although he couldn't move around much, he kept me hopping. I always had to be ready for his next interruption. If he interrupted work with play, I turned the play into work.

One memorable night, we made chocolate chip cookies to practice fractions and discuss physical and chemical changes. I made him measure fractions of cups, then I had him calculate the whole recipe in teaspoons. Afterward we counted the number of cookies, each made from a teaspoonful of dough. Why weren't they equal? That stopped him for awhile. That night, I stayed ahead. (And that night, he dreamed about fractions.)

As much as I loved him, I worried about him. He

was very bright, but didn't think as most people do. Instead of reasoning in a straight line (A to B), he visualized the whole concept and then meandered around ideas until he reached a conclusion (A to W to T to B). Such thinking is not welcomed in most schools, and Eddie paid for it. He made it through by the skin of his teeth.

His mother and I talked about this occasionally. She was concerned, but once said, "I think he'll turn out all right."

She was right.

During his summers, Eddie learned to work hard. Since finishing high school, he's worked hard at many jobs and his diligence has paid off.

Eddie is now in his thirties, the manager of a camera store. He's married. And he's a home owner. Thinking of Eddie fills me with pride—and hope.

His success tells me you should never give up on a child. It also reminds me that there is more to life than school and books, and that character comes from hard work.

Those days when my kids drive me up a wall with their interruptions and problems, I think of Eddie.

And I know that in time they, too, will turn out all right.

Father, if I do nothing else for my children,
let me make them accountable so they learn
to do their work diligently.
Thank You for filling the world with Eddies—
kids who don't fit the mold,
but fit into Your perfect plan.

Let your conversation be without covetousness;
and be content with such things
as ye have: for he hath said,
I will never leave thee, nor forsake thee.
HEBREWS 13:5

Benjamin came bouncing into the living room.

He struck a pose with his arms outstretched and smiled.

"How do you like me?" (Translation: "How do you like my outfit?")

I looked him over as I do each morning. Shirt and pants didn't clash. Shoes on. So far so good.

But then I noticed something amiss. His pants were bulging oddly.

"What's wrong with your pants? Come here."

As he ran to me, I could see that the tiny pockets in his shorts, which were meant more for fashion than function, were about to burst.

"See what's in my pah-its?" he said.

He squeezed his left hand into the left pocket and tugged and tugged. Out came a two-inch bouncy ball.

"See, my ball." The hand went back.

"And *t'ree* pennies!"

The right hand went into the right pocket once—"a bouncy ball"—and again, this time slowly, with a little flourish—"my B'UE marbowl!" His eyes sparkled.

"Wow!" I said, "you sure have a lot in those pockets!"

"Yeah!" he beamed. He gathered his treasures and refilled his pockets.

As he ran back to his room, I had to smile. There went a kid after my own heart, one who loved pockets.

I've loved pockets as long as I can remember. When I was a little older than Ben I hated dresses because most didn't have pockets. In high school, my favorite pants were paint pants that had a pocket on the leg and a hammer loop. Even now I'd rather wear a full skirt with pockets than a formfitting skirt without them.

What amused me more than Ben's liking for pockets was his love for the stuff in them. He truly had "kid pockets" full of the simple things—balls, marbles, pennies—that make a kid's life content.

Lucky kid! He had a pocket full of happiness.

I envied him.

Some time ago, I traded kid pockets for adult ones.

And now I have mother pockets, filled with responsibilities. In them I find a packet of vital ID cards, keys, and—maybe—a little cash. Sometimes I might find a tissue to wipe little noses, or a Band-Aid, paper clip, or rubber band for various projects or emergencies.

Sometimes I wish I could empty those pockets. But I can't.

But nothing is stopping me from adding to them.

The next orphaned marble I find goes in mine.

Forgive me, Father, for always wanting so much.
Let me learn to be content with the simple things in life,
knowing that I have all I need because I have You.

For as the heavens are higher than the earth,
so are my ways higher than your ways,
and my thoughts than your thoughts.
ISAIAH 55:9

Ben was standing on a bag of building tiles, snooping in my drawer of pictures.

He leaned forward just enough to shift the center of gravity. The blocks tipped and off he slipped!

"WHEE!" he said.

"Whoops!" I said.

He stood up and faced me.

"No, Mommy," he said soberly, "that was a 'whee' not a 'whoops.' "

"Maybe for you," I said. "For me, it was a 'whoops.' "

He's not the first kid to have an opinion different from his mother's. In fact, he's from a long line of kids who think differently.

His siblings have enjoyed climbing on roofs, in trees, and up waterfalls. They've been thrilled dropping through space on roller coasters. They've dared gravity by standing on their heads with only a thin rug to protect their backs from a concrete floor.

They call these things "fun."

I call them "foolish."

It's all a matter of perspective. Parents see things children cannot.

So it is with God.

When I encounter a difficult time, I begin to whine: "It's too hard, Father. I'm not strong enough for this crisis."

And He says:

> *My grace is sufficient for thee:*
> *for my strength is made perfect in weakness.*
> 2 CORINTHIANS 12:9

Supper is burning, the baby is crying, the math lesson is missing, and my long-suffering is long gone. "Why does it all happen at once?!" I scream.

And He says:

> *The trying of your faith worketh patience.*
> JAMES 1:3

I get up early to work, struggle to write all day, then stay up late to make a deadline. I think this is fulfillment.

But He says:

> *It is vain for you to rise up early, to sit up late,*
> *to eat the bread of sorrows:*
> *for I give my beloved sleep.*
> PSALM 127:2 (PARAPHRASED)

I look in the children's closets and fret. "How can I afford clothes for everyone?"

And He says:

> *If I clothe the grass of the field, which today is,*
> *and tomorrow is cast into the oven,*
> *shall I not much more clothe you,*
> *O ye of little faith?*
> MATTHEW 6:30 (PARAPHRASED)

God's perspective is so different from mine. What I consider a trial, He sees as a blessing. When I think I'm a spiritual giant, He knows I'm but a foolish child.

Often I look at my foolish children and think, "Someday you will understand."

And His voice inside echoes: "Someday, so will you."

. . .

Lord, *open my eyes;*
give me Your perspective on life.
Let me see my life as You see it,
so I can please You and bring You glory.

FINDING GOD
IN LIFE'S COMMON EXPERIENCES. . .

*Where is God when an airplane crashes,
when the house is falling apart on Sunday
mornings, when a child is sick, when dreams
are dashed? Can we see Him when we're stuck
on the road with a flat tire, or when we're
waiting in a slow express line? We can if we're
willing to look.*

As the hart panteth after the water brooks,
so panteth my soul after thee, O God.
PSALM 42:1

Every Sunday it's the same.
No matter how well organized I am, the morning gets chaotic.

It's the morning I invariably burn the bagels and the kids smear jelly on the funnies.

On Sunday my paperboys go back to bed and oversleep, while the preschoolers get up too early. And no matter when they rise, they are all crabby.

Some time between sunset Saturday and sunrise Sunday, my kids' shoes come to life—and walk away. Sunday is the day sandals vanish, to reappear miraculously—after church. Sunday is the day the water heater leaks and the chicken pox hatch.

And Sunday is the day the baby just has to burp bananas all over my dress, usually as we are going out the door!

I'm not alone. The Sunday Meltdown Syndrome affects most churchgoing families I know, even those with fewer children and better-organized mothers.

Why?

Some say it's all Satan's doing, to keep us from worshipping God. That's reasonable, but let's not give him more credit than he deserves. He and his hellish henchmen may affect circumstances, but they don't control my reactions.

I am also responsible. For some reason, I expect things that don't go right the rest of the week to go right on Sunday, and when they don't, I get annoyed.

And don't rule out God's hand—He allows Sunday Meltdown. He must have a good reason. If nothing else, when things melt down, I am more inclined to look up, to see how much I need Him.

God's also in the business of making beauty from ashes. He can and does use the chaos of Sunday for my benefit and His glory.

Because when I finally get to church, breathless and panting, I know for certain it's where I need to be.

. . .

Dear Father, in the midst of chaos I cry to You.
Hear my voice. Let me see You as You are.
You are high and exalted and able to lift me
above my circumstances so I can worship You.

And he commanded the multitude
to sit down on the ground.
MATTHEW 15:35

Back in the dark ages, when I was a child,
it was thought a good thing that children learn to sit.
I had to sit in school (with hands folded on my desk),
at the table (with hands in my lap), and in the car
(keeping my hands to myself).

And of course, I sat in church.

From the time I was wrapped in blankets, I was
taken to church. There was no question in the minds
of my parents that I could sit; there was no doubt that
I should sit; it was just accepted that I would sit.

Without the slightest notion that I was being
repressed by an authoritarian figure or indoctrinated
with my parents' religious beliefs against my will, I
happily went to church and sat. With minimal fidget-
ing. Through the Most Boring Sermons of All Time.
Week after week after week.

My, how times have changed!

Now that I am grown, society doesn't expect children to sit. School desks have been replaced by mats
on the floor; table manners go untaught; and cars
have been replaced by vans big enough to separate siblings and reduce the need for self-control.

And of course, sitting in church is definitely not expected. Babies and toddlers go to nursery; older children

to "Children's Church." And now—surprise, surprise—churches are full of ten year olds who can't sit still.

In recent years, however, I've noticed more parents are once again teaching their young children to sit in church. I welcome this, because I hate being alone in the struggle.

And it is a struggle. Little ones do not naturally sit—they need constant encouragement to be still. Yet it is not unnatural to teach them to do so. It is good for them to learn self-control, and the earlier, the better.

The sooner a child learns to sit and listen in church, the sooner he will learn to sit and listen to God on his own. From sitting in church, he will also learn to respect, revere, and worship God.

Sitting before God anywhere has its own blessings. God communicates with still hearts. Christ worked two great miracles after the people sat down. When Mary sat at Jesus' feet, He said she had chosen the good part.

It is still a good thing for children of all ages to sit. Still good to be still.

My tendency is to run, Father,
to do two or more things at once.
Yet I find You want all my attention, all my worship.
I can only do this when I'm quiet and still.
Teach me the discipline of stillness,
and give me the wisdom and determination I need
to teach it to my little ones.

For now we see through a glass, darkly;
but then face to face: now I know in part;
but then shall I know even as also I am known.
1 Corinthians 13:12

Sometimes life hurts.

It especially hurts when there is pain but no answer for it.

Take, for example, the death of the young, those we think are not supposed to die.

Not many years ago, our family lost a cousin in a car accident.

Her name was Susan, and she was just nineteen. She was pretty, bright, and friendly, the kind of daughter every parent would love to claim. She was on her way to a college in upstate New York to study aeronautics. Someday, she wanted to be an astronaut.

More than ten years ago, I knew another nineteen year old. Her name was Betsy, and she was pretty, bright, and friendly, the kind of kid every parent would love to claim. She was an engineering major going into her sophomore year at Colorado State University. Someday, she would fly military aircraft.

But one July day while on a training flight, something happened. Betsy's plane fell out of the sky. And Betsy, a friend said, "just flew away."

More than twenty-five years ago, there was a young

man in my hometown named Paul. He was clean-cut, intelligent, and funny, the kind of son every parent would love to claim. In his junior year of high school, he decided that someday he would be a minister.

A few short weeks after that decision, he and two friends were overcome by mine gas in the cellar of a hunting cabin.

For Susan, Betsy, and Paul there were no Somedays. And for their families and friends, there was only a question: Why?

Why are young people, who have so much ambition and so much potential, taken away?

There is an answer, but the One who holds it is also the One who said, "my ways (are) higher than your ways and my thoughts than your thoughts."

We proud humans are often offended when God withholds knowledge. We hurt because we cannot know now.

But our hope is that someday we will.

. . .

Father, *I cannot hope to understand*
Your infinite wisdom that allows the death of
young people who have so much potential.
Yet I must yield to Your sovereignty,
knowing Your ways are higher than mine.
I look forward to the time when I will truly understand.

And he said unto them,
Come ye yourselves apart into a desert place,
and rest a while:
for there were many coming and going,
and they had no leisure so much as to eat.
MARK 6:31

For thirty-eight of my forty-three years, I lived with winter.

I grew up near the coal regions of Pennsylvania where, according to my uncles, there were only two seasons—winter and the Fourth of July.

Since leaving Pennsylvania I've lived in southern Illinois (milder winters, but snow still possible), in the foothills of the Colorado Rockies (more frequent snow, but didn't last long), in the snowbelt of central New York (continual snow cover from November until April), in Maine (hadn't seen a good Maine winter in years—until we showed up), and in South Dakota (slogan: "Cold faces, cold places.").

I have thick coal-cracker blood, a permanent layer of insulation around my thighs and waist, and an ankle that predicts winter storms.

And I'm married to a weatherman, a guy who looks at colorful computerized maps and says such happy things as, "There's no warm air in the foreseeable future."

Given all this, why was I never ready for winter?

I knew it was going to come. I knew the coats,

boots, scarves, hats, and mittens needed to be retrieved, cleaned, sorted, and assigned. I knew the shorts needed to be replaced with the corduroys.

I knew it. Why then couldn't I do the job before the cold struck?

When it came to winter, I lived in denial. I overlooked the significance of red leaves, October calendar pages, Christmas displays. If I didn't think about it, I didn't have to deal with it.

Our last fall in South Dakota, however, I really did try. I washed mittens, hats, and coats throughout the summer. But then October came and it was warm and instead of dealing with the winter clothes, I painted the house.

Then the clock changed, and suddenly the sky was dark by supper time, and it was cold again. And I wasn't ready.

Sigh.

It's not that I don't like winter. I do like the season; I think we need it. Winter imposes a certain quietness; it gives us time to rest, to reflect.

Winter puts life in perspective. Without the chill and death of winter, would we really appreciate the warmth and rebirth of spring?

Living on Guam, a land of perpetual summer, I miss winter. The year never pauses. Neither do I.

Yes, winter is good for the soul.

Even if a soul isn't ready.

Father, I appreciate those times of rest and barrenness
You sometimes force upon us.
Let me welcome them as gifts from You,
knowing that You are with me
in the desert places as much as You
are with me in the green pastures.

While the earth remaineth,
seedtime and harvest, and cold and heat,
and summer and winter,
and day and night shall not cease.

GENESIS 8:22

I've seen some impressive winters.

New York snowbelt, permafrost winters with more than 120 inches of snow. And Maine winters complete with nor'easters. I've driven white-knuckled through lake-effect whiteouts. I have fought the ravages of storms and snowplows with a single shovel.

But I never saw a winter like the South Dakota winter of 1996–97.

It had a life of its own.

It was voracious. It engulfed houses and ate up streets and cars and lives. Its white, sticky tentacles wrapped around us, jealously defending us from spring. Even after spring prevailed for a spell, the winter monster would not die. It came back in April, howling angrily as it pounced on motorists and knocked out power.

The last battle left many frustrated. The talk around town was tinged with weariness.

"I'm ready for it to be over."

"I've had enough."

"Will it ever end?"

The hopeful smiles of spring turned to heavy sighs.

Even my weatherman was ready to quit. In March, he had tolled winter's death knell. Three weeks later, he spent hours watching its resurrection and shoveling through its discarded shroud. He consoled himself: "This is just a glitch in the increasing temperature trend." (In other words, he had made a boo-boo.)

Even the children had had it. The delighted choruses of "Mommy!! It's snowing!!!" turned into dirges— "It's snowing. . .again. . . ."

Still, the last storm cloud had a silver lining, and it was in its victims. We Dakotans showed our mettle. Neighbors helped neighbors; strangers helped strangers. We fought it nobly—and found our greatness again.

And we again saw our weakness. Although we can plow through it and sandbag against it, we cannot control nature. To endure it gracefully, we must submit to the One who can.

A three-year-old friend, Carolyn, taught me this.

"Dear God," she prayed after the storm, "make our snow go away and keep the water out of our basement."

Amen, Carolyn.
Amen.

Lessons for a Supermom

It's in the winters of life
I come to know You better, Father.
Give me patience to endure the trials
that never seem to end,
knowing that You are controlling the circumstances
in my life to teach me the lessons
You want me to learn.
Spring will come, for so You have promised.

Casting all your care upon him;
for he careth for you.
1 PETER 5:7

I used to worry a lot.

I worried about schoolwork, about riding public transportation, about being an old maid. I worried that Mike's plane would go down in a typhoon; that my babies would be ugly.

Name a subject, I could worry about it.

Thankfully, as I've become older, I've become less anxious. Besides, worry is a waste of precious time. So I don't fret as much as I used to.

But when I do—I do it big.

Take the weekend Matthew went camping on short notice. When I said, "You may go," I was thinking about food, not about the dangers of camping.

Later at supper, a thought overcame me: a camping accident; Matthew would be seriously hurt—or worse.

I tried to shake the feeling but couldn't. What if he were hurt or killed? What would I do? I hadn't taken his picture in months—what could I show people?

I fed the baby mechanically as I fought tears thinking of lost hugs and laughs, and of regrets for my many mistakes. My countenance fell.

"Honey," Mike said, "are you all right?"

"No. I just had a bad feeling. Matthew is going to get hurt."

Mike, who distrusts feelings, was unmoved. "He's probably in more danger playing soccer than camping. He'll be fine. Just trust God."

Leave it to a man to derail a four-star worry! Annoyed by his logic, I left the table. He was right; still I was fearful. Finally I prayed and the fear dissipated.

"Worry," someone told me, "is taking on a responsibility God never intended you to have."

When we worry, we think God is not able to control a situation or care for our loved ones. Worry is faithlessness; it's a sin.

But it's not without benefit. Thinking about the what-ifs make me more appreciative of the what-ares.

Matthew came home excited—and intact.

I hugged him. And then I took his picture.

. . .

Lord, forgive me for holding onto my worries
and not trusting that You can
deal with them better than I.
Let me have confidence in You,
knowing that I am safe in Your hand.

And to knowledge temperance;
and to temperance patience;
and to patience godliness.
2 PETER 1:6

I sat on the emergency room gurney, holding John, my redheaded toddler.

With each rapid, shallow breath came a squeaky wheeze. He sounded like a sick accordion.

As I rubbed his back, I thought back to the many hours I spent on the couch as a child, struggling for a breath, while Mom rubbed my back, both of us wishing for relief. I thought of summers spent in air conditioning, out of the reach of pollen and heat; of pushing a bike, not riding it; of spending gym class on the sidelines.

"I'm sorry I've given you the asthma, John," I whispered to him. "But, trust me, this will develop character."

As I've considered those words over the years, I've realized their prophetic nature, and not just for John. Certainly, he is a determined, brave, and resilient child. But I, too, have developed character. Not so much from John's asthma, but from the emergency-room experience. Going to the ER has taught me many things:

— Humility: Before I walk into an ER, I have to admit that I alone cannot care for my child.

This is a very humbling experience for a person who thinks of herself as resourceful and able.

— Knowledge: I've learned a lot about asthma protocols over the years. From this I've been able to help other parents of asthmatics.

— Patience: It's amazing how long one sometimes has to wait in an "emergency" situation. They don't call us "patients" for nothing. Through waiting, God has had many opportunities to develop temperance and graciousness within me.

— Wisdom: Sometimes it is necessary for a mother to exercise her rightful control over her own child, even if it appears foolish to the medical professionals. In emergencies, God gives the necessary discernment.

— Faith: In every crisis, faith has been tested. Each time, God has shown Himself faithful. I've also had my faith in other people tested. And most times, it has been kept intact. People are still made in the image of God; in a crisis, most still respond as He would.

— Thankfulness: When an emergency is over, it's easy to be thankful. But God has taught me to be thankful in the crisis, because He is there to take me through it.

Each time we go to the ER, God teaches these lessons.

Given the number of trips, I must be a slower learner than I thought.

. . .

Although I have not desired to have
so many opportunities to learn patience,
all these crises have developed patience, temperance,
and, perhaps, a little godliness.
For that I'm thankful, Father.
Even so, I pray You will protect my children
from their own foolishness.

And the world passeth away,
and the lust thereof:
but he that doeth the will of God
abideth for ever.
1 JOHN 2:17

One day I went into the Black Hole.

The Black Hole is my office. It is a repository for anything anyone wants to drop there. Kids' books needing repair. Legos. Receipts. Mail. Name it. You're apt to find it—or lose it—in the Black Hole.

This day the stuff hit critical mass, the point when I can no longer stand it. I began shoveling out the Black Hole.

It's the toughest job in the house. Although it doesn't take much energy to repair books and file receipts, it takes my every drop of resolve to dispose of an unread magazine or newsletter.

That's because I'm an information junkie. I like to be informed. Therefore, I must read everything the mail carrier drops through the slot.

But I can't. There are not enough uninterrupted hours in my day to process all the information that bombards me.

If the printed media are too much, imagine how the Internet complicates things. An instant response is inherent in the nature of electronic mail. The Internet itself is a sea of information that can drown even the skilled web-surfer.

I can't handle any more!

And maybe I shouldn't.

Others I know are having similar thoughts—and they're fighting back.

One friend refuses to own a computer. He doesn't have an answering machine. All unsolicited mail gets piled on his desk unopened. When the pile gets too high, he tosses it into the wood stove and burns it.

Another friend gave away her television and canceled her newspaper. Now she says she is less stressed.

This is not a matter of hiding one's head in the sand. It's a matter of keeping one's heart out of the world. There is wisdom in it.

When I get to the end of my life, will I regret not having read the September 1997 issue of *Macuser*? No. But I may regret not having read to my toddlers.

Again, it's priorities. Read magazines for my enlightenment or Laura Ingalls Wilder for their enjoyment? Spend time shuffling papers or putting pictures into albums?

The world can—and will—go on without my constant scrutiny. But my family can't.

So I'm making a declaration: I will no longer be tyrannized by information and clutter!

I'd put that in writing, too, but I left my pen in the Black Hole.

Father, the temptation is so great to know the world,
to be of it more than just in it.
Help me to sort through the clutter of information
to find only what I need to know to be wise,
so I can declare Your truth to this generation.
If I am faced with a choice,
remind me that I can never go wrong
choosing Your Word over the words of the world.

Delight thyself also in the LORD;
and he shall give thee the desires of thine heart.
PSALM 37:4

I stood at the recycler's for nearly an hour, ripping up a dream.

With sad resolve, I tore the covers off several hundred copies of a publication I had produced ten years earlier. As I did, I watched a dream dissolve.

Rip!

I can't believe I'm doing this. This was my baby, my great idea. Why am I throwing it away?

Rip!

It was a good idea—a handbook to teach the Ladies of the Clubs how to deal with irascible reporters and editors. But I've waited too long to market it—it's out-of-date.

Toss.

Maybe there is still a market. But can I find it? Will I find it? Yes, but probably not.

Rip!

I've lugged two hundred pounds of paper and ink from New York to Maine to South Dakota, hoping for that elusive "someday" when I'd be able to sell them. The someday hasn't come.

Rip!

You have to make "somedays;" they don't just happen.

Toss.

One day I'll have time to make a "someday." Today I have other things to do.

Rip!

Recyling workers offer to help.

"No, thank you." I have to do the job myself. Besides, Rip! the cover stock is still good. The kids can use it for scratch.

Toss.

Why all this agony? Other people have lost their dreams; I'm not the first.

Rip!

Mom dreamed of writing a book, but she was always too busy to write.

Rip!

Debbie dreamed of getting well, but she didn't.

Pause.

Some people don't have the privilege of ripping up their dreams. Some dreams are ripped off; others, ripped away. My nephew's dream for his life and education has been suddenly altered by leukemia.

Give helper a stack for the bin. I can recycle the paper—and the dream. As long as I'm breathing, I can think and create. Maybe it won't sell, but the greater joy is in the creation.

Rip!

One dream down; a zillion more to go.

Let my dreams be Your dreams, Father.
Put Your desires in me so they become mine.
Let my dreams soar as high as You will take them,
beyond all I can ask or think.
But always keep my feet planted on the sin-cursed ground,
to remind me that You are the only One who
does all things well.

Is there any thing whereof it may be said,
See, this is new?
it hath been already of old time,
which was before us.
ECCLESIASTES 1:10

It was a dark, but clear, night on Guam.

The road, full of potholes and twists, was all but deserted. The light from my tiny Toyota lit the tree-lined road like a flashlight. Beyond the beam, foreboding blackness.

Suddenly, a shrill scream! And another! And another!

"Please, Baby, please. Don't cry." I patted his leg. "We'll be home soon."

But nothing would calm one-month-old Matthew. He was unhappy. Very unhappy.

I was a new mother, full of determination and lofty ideals. And I was frustrated. Despite the fact I was doing everything Mom would have wanted me to do for her first grandson—breastfeeding him and keeping him away from disposable diapers and pacifiers—he was not perfect.

And I was going to be the perfect first-time mommy. I was going to treat him like a second-born and not sweat the small stuff. But I was sweating.

I couldn't help him. I couldn't nurse, and it was too dangerous to pull the car over to change his cloth diaper. I had no pacifier; I didn't believe in them.

He continued to scream. I thought the car windows would shatter.

My frustration grew with every wail. I could do nothing to shut him up. I was ready to cry myself.

I found myself doing the only thing I could do: "Please, Lord," I prayed, "make him quiet. What have I done? Please calm him down. Give me patience— now! Please get me home safely."

He did. As soon as I got Matthew out of the car seat, he stopped fussing!

Sixteen years later, I found myself driving a fifteen-passenger van on a dark, bumpy Guam road with Mom's last grandchild. Although nursed and usually in cloth diapers, she had just finished a bottle and was in a disposable diaper. The pacifier was at home, along with the diaper bag.

And she was crying. And crying. And crying.

"She smells," her big sister said.

I could do nothing. Again caught in an impossible situation, I again found myself praying. "Lord, why did I come out without an extra diaper? By now I should know better. Forgive me, Father. Please calm her. Please get us home safely."

He did.

When I got her out of the car seat she stopped fussing!

Sigh.

There's nothing really new under the sun.

The more things change, the more they remain the same.

. . .

The hearts of mothers and babies never change,
do they, Father?
No matter where we are stuck with a fussy baby,
we are all stuck in our flesh.
Still, the impossible situations make me turn to You.
But please give me the wisdom to avoid them as best I can.

Weeping may endure for a night,
but joy cometh in the morning.
Psalm 30:5

A night was never darker than the night we left Aberdeen, South Dakota.

With good-byes said and house cleaned, we shut the door on Kline Street. As we drove down the alley that last time, I was determined to not look back.

But behind me, little faces could not help it. Their breathless sobs and tearstained cheeks troubled me.

Why were we taking them from their friends? From a safe and comfortable place? Taking them to a little island in a big ocean?

Why?

It wasn't a question I could answer easily for myself, let alone explain to them. We were going because this was Daddy's dream job. Because we were a family, it was our dream, too.

And there was something more—a deep, inexpressible conviction that God was leading us back to Guam.

Besides, we couldn't stay. I had given away the winter clothes.

Still, it was difficult. But it was right.

Yet as the last lights of Aberdeen disappeared, I wondered. And as the cries in the back were engulfed by sleep, I feared what lay beyond the darkness.

To our amazement, the sun came up the next morning! With it came new hope for our new life.

Though we didn't know all that was ahead, the way was brighter, the hearts lighter. We knew we could make it. And by God's grace, we did.

As I've thought about that first night, I've heard my mother's voice. "It's always darkest before the dawn," she'd say. In other words, you don't know light until you've experienced darkness; you won't know joy until you've suffered.

It's the Easter principle. Darkness gives way to light. Sorrow to joy. Death to life.

This principle applies in little ways throughout life. But it applied once in a great way two thousand years ago.

Jesus Christ—that provocative prophet whose words cut like a sword—was dead, crucified by the very people He had come to save.

But three days later, as He had promised, He was alive again! Death was swallowed up in life! Because of the death and resurrection of the Holy man, sinful men could live forever.

Because of His journey through darkness, our hearts are brighter. We can make it.

And by God's grace we will.

Father, thank You for the victory I have in Christ.
Because of Him,
I know there is morning on the other side of night
and joy on the other side of sorrow.
He has wiped the tears from my eyes
to let me see the hope that lies before me.

The Lord is good to all:
and his tender mercies are over all his works.
PSALM 145:9

One Sunday while driving home from church with Matthew, the tire blew out.

I assessed the situation: Hot day. Flat tire. My best church dress. High heels. Matthew in his best trousers. Neither of us was fit for the job at hand.

Yet as I reached for the door handle, I thought, "This is good."

Ordinarily, I wouldn't have thought that, but that morning in Sunday school, a friend had shared this story:

> *A king had a loyal and faithful cupbearer. The king trusted him completely. The two were friends. But the cupbearer had an interesting habit. In the most dire circumstances, his first response was always to say, "This is good."*
>
> *One day, the king had a black-powder rifle. The cupbearer loaded it incorrectly and when it fired, it blew off the king's thumb. The cupbearer said, "This is good." Enraged, the king threw his friend into the deepest dungeon.*
>
> *A year later, the king was traveling in Africa when a tribe of man-eaters captured him. As he was about to be cooked, the tribe's*

leader noticed he had no thumb. Because they would not eat anything imperfect, the king was released.

He hurried home and to the dungeon. He was filled with overwhelming thankfulness, for he realized that had he not lost his thumb, he would have lost his life. The king released his friend and could not apologize enough for having imprisoned him.

All the cupbearer said was: "This is good; this is good."

"How can you say that being locked in a dungeon was good?!" the king demanded.

"Sire," the cupbearer said, "I am your cupbearer. I am always at your side. Had I not been in prison, I would have surely been with you when they discovered your thumb missing. I would have been eaten instead. So this is good."

My friend's story demonstrated that even the apparent tragedies of life are good because they come from the hand of a Father who is infinitely good and works all things together for our good.

Before we had jacked up the car, a man approached us carrying a lug wrench. He removed the tire, repaired the spare, and got us on the road within ten minutes.

In time, God may use us to bless this man, and

that will be good for him.
God really is good.
Even when tires go bad.

. . .

I say it in my head,
but help me know it in my heart:
God is good. Knowing this,
let me remember that all things that come
through Your hands are eventually good,
because You cause all things to work together for good.
Let me not despise the bad things in life,
rather let me accept them graciously,
knowing that Your mercy is over all Your works.

And he answering said,
Thou shalt love the Lord thy God
with all thy heart,
and with all thy soul,
and with all thy strength,
and with all thy mind;
and thy neighbour as thyself.
LUKE 10:27

Toward the end of my last pregnancy, I became a couch potato.

I was on modified bed rest because "Hallie" was not moving enough. Part of this inactivity was related to decreased amniotic fluid.

To help the situation, I was as inactive as possible. I camped out on the couch.

Being stuck on the couch gave me a new perspective on life.

From my couch I could see a tropical world. Through a dirty sliding door, I saw coconut palms nodding in the breeze, a deep blue sky, billowy white clouds. I saw grass that grew faster than lawn boys could mow.

Inside that glass door I saw ants, too many of them, running helter-skelter over my living room floor.

Beneath a chair were socks, books, and puzzle pieces. In the corners, I saw dust rabbits (they were bigger than bunnies), lost pens, and rubber bands.

And because I was "resting," I did nothing about any of it.

Life went on, even when the floor was dirty.

And life went on, even without me.

Little people ran to and fro before me, busy with a hundred important things—building block houses, making pictures, reading books, performing magic tricks.

Big boys did dishes.

And the husband shopped for groceries.

On the couch, I was humbled. All those things I thought must be done my way didn't really need to be done at all sometimes. We really could live if the wash wasn't done on schedule and the beds weren't made.

Lying on the couch was good for my circulation, but it was better for my soul.

From there, I saw that the most important things in life were not things at all. People were most important.

When I was on the couch, I encountered those people anew. Suddenly, I was at their level. And they took every advantage. They brought books to read, games to play.

So I read and played. And felt a twinge of guilt for not doing more of that when life was normal.

One evening while resting, Ben ran to me, stuck his face in mine and said, "I need give you a tiss." He hugged and kissed me and ran off giggling.

On the couch, I saw life wasn't perfect.

But it was still very, very good.

. . .

Thank You for reminding me that
I need to love the little "neighbors"
You have put at my feet,
within my own house.
Let me never push them aside for the sake of
an object or activity.
Being flat on my back helps me look up at You
and around at all You have given me.
You are so generous, Father.
I am not worthy of the goodness You bestow.

He hath made every thing beautiful in his time:
also he hath set the world in their heart,
so that no man can find out the work that
God maketh from the beginning to the end.
ECCLESIASTES 3:11

In contrast to the natural beauty that abounds on Guam,

we have some not-so-beautiful man-made additions. Most disgracefully, we have a problem with graffiti.

It's such a problem, retailers can't sell spray paint to anyone under eighteen.

One village mayor came up with a proactive solution. Instead of letting vandals deface his retaining walls, he had students paint murals on them.

An art class from the university had the longest wall. Their mural—a montage of island and sea life—is more than one hundred feet long.

I was fascinated watching this mural develop.

In one weekend, the plain wall became a blueprint. The whole design was outlined in blue by a few dozen students—flowers, jungle animals, sea creatures were all there, waiting to be filled in.

The students were so fast, I expected the mural would be completed the next weekend. But no. The actual painting was done by a handful of artists who worked a few hours every day all summer long.

They worked carefully and methodically, from

north to south. Occasionally, one painter moved ahead a few feet. Then out of the sea of white jumped a somber brown carabao or a stunning red blossom. It stayed there alone for awhile, then gradually was enveloped by the rest of the picture.

Gradually, the mural blossomed. It took more than six months, but we now have a new, beautiful man-made attraction on our island.

While the mural is a delight to my eyes, it's also become a lesson for my soul.

Just as I saw the whole plan of the mural, God, who mysteriously lives beyond time, saw the whole plan of my life before I was born. Like the artists, He outlined the circumstances of my life and the works I will do.

And now I must carefully fill in the picture. I can paint the mosaic of my life in bright or warm colors, or drab browns and blacks. I can use calm, smooth strokes, or bold, agitated ones.

But unlike the mural, I cannot see the whole picture of my life. From my earthly perspective, it sometimes seems to be random splotches of color, like carrot stains on a white blouse.

Yet when I get to heaven and God shows me the big picture He's been painting in my life, I know I'll be amazed.

Because God makes all things beautiful in His time.

Even carrot stains on a white blouse.

I praise You, Father,
because You know the end from the beginning,
and You see it all at once.
Although I sometimes can't see beyond my nose,
I know that You know where I'm going.
Help me have the patience to
let You take me there in Your time.

And we know that all things work together
for good to them that love God,
to them who are the called
according to his purpose.
ROMANS 8:28

When I looked in my sons' room early on
October 26, 1999, I wasn't fully awake.

Their radio was blaring, so I poked my head in the door.

The oldest, Matthew, was sitting at his desk staring at his algebra book.

"What's up?"

"Payne Stewart died in a plane crash," he said sadly.

"Who's Payne Stewart?" Somehow I sensed it was a "stupid" question.

"He was a great golfer," Matthew said graciously. "I followed him in the sports pages. . . . It was near Aberdeen."

Now I was wide awake.

"Aberdeen, South Dakota?"

"That's what they said."

Suddenly, his sadness became mine. While I did not know Payne Stewart, I did know Aberdeen. I've driven through Mina, where the plane came down. Mike and the boys camped near Mina Lake. My daughters' bunk bed came from a house on the lakefront.

I could picture the wreckage in a flat, open field of yellowing fall grass. I could see shocked bystanders in green John Deere caps and blue jeans, all frustrated because they could not help.

Hearing this happened near Aberdeen changed everything. Knowing the crash would affect the good people of South Dakota transformed it from a news story to a very real tragedy. My concern for my son's feelings became sorrow for the survivors.

I delayed breakfast to review wire stories on the Internet. I read that Mr. Stewart was a Christian. Certainly God had guided the plane, which had flown for several hours on autopilot, over many populated areas to an empty field in South Dakota. Because God was there, this tragedy was not for nothing.

And no tragedy ever is, especially one that befalls a child of God. This is because absolutely nothing comes upon us without the Father's knowledge. All things— the good and the bad—fit within His divine plan. He causes all things to work together for the good.

Who knows what good will come from this calamity? Perhaps some will read of Mr. Stewart's faith and desire to know his God; perhaps a child will be inspired to excel in golf. Maybe somebody will make improvements in small jets, or invent an autopilot that can be overridden from a remote location.

Maybe a humbled onlooker will go home and hug his kid. Maybe a hotshot reporter will finally realize that public figures deserve a private moment and will put down his mike and cry.

Only God knows.

And in that we can trust, even though we do not understand.

. . .

Father, there are no true surprises in my life.
Though situations may surprise me,
You are never astonished.
And You work all these things into a glorious plan
to conform me to the image of Christ.
Please use this "tragedy" to
transform lives across the globe,
and comfort those who were left behind.

Wherefore we receiving a kingdom
which cannot be moved,
let us have grace,
whereby we may serve God acceptably
with reverence and godly fear.
HEBREWS 12:28

June 29, 2000

We had an earthquake tonight!

Make that earthquakes. We had at least four!

Earthquakes on Guam do not usually make headlines. While there was a major quake within the last ten years, most quakes here just shake the windows and rumble the concrete floors. Thankfully, they do little structural damage.

But they are tough on the nerves.

Tonight's series of shakes and aftershocks had the whole house in a panic.

I was changing the baby when I sensed the first one, which lasted the better part of a minute. The floor started shaking. I finished diapering her as I yelled, "Earthquake!"

That was unnecessary. The children were already running for the door. No sooner were we out than the phone rang. It was Mike calling from work to make sure we were okay.

A few minutes later, there was a slight aftershock, which didn't bother anyone. But within fifteen minutes, we had another window-shaker. Again we went outside. And within an hour of this one, there was another mild one, which went unnoticed by most of the children.

When life started settling down, the children started thinking about the experience.

"I wonder why God is sending all these earthquakes," Charles said.

"Maybe it's because He wants to send us a trial," Thomas replied.

"Maybe He wants to show us who's in control," someone said.

Later, Matthew came in.

"Actually, I was kind of expecting this," he said. "We haven't had a good one since February. The plates actually build up pressure that they need to release."

"Oh, earth plates are like mothers," I said.

He just gave me a sixteen-year-old look and walked away.

The quake was even on the toddler's mind.

"Affer we go to bed," Ben asked, "will there be another earfquake?"

"I hope not," I said.

Earthquakes, however mild, are unnerving. When a concrete floor feels like Jell-O, I tend to get a little weak in the knees. Then the best place to be is on my knees.

If God wanted to make a point tonight, He succeeded. He moved earth to show me that He is the

One in control, that He holds the power.

As for me, I need to stop living my life in my own strength, on my own feet.

And start living it in His strength, on my knees.

. . .

Though my world can get shaken at times,
I know I stand on a solid rock.
Thank You for reminding me that my strength alone
is inadequate to uphold me.
You are my strength.

Who knowing the judgment of God,
that they which commit such things
are worthy of death, not only do the same,
but have pleasure in them that do them.

ROMANS 1:32

Beneath the sale tent, the bargains were plenteous;

the shoppers, tenacious; the checkout lines, disastrous.

For hundreds of bargain-hungry shoppers, the management had only set up three checkout stands. Two were open to all; the third was limited to twelve items and cash.

I had two items and a checkbook, but I did not have the patience for the longer line. So I returned one item and got in the shorter, cash-only express line.

And there I stayed for forty-five minutes.

The problem was twofold. First, the checker was unfamiliar with the products and prices, so she was looking up nearly every item. Second, of the dozen shoppers ahead of me, I saw only one who was obviously within the item limit.

The worst offenders were right in front of me. Knowing the wait was long, the husband and children stood in line with the cart while the wife ran about finding stuff to fill it. Even after the husband weakly pointed out she had exceeded the limit, she kept shopping.

How rude!

With each new item that landed in their cart, my temperature went up a degree. By the time I got to the checkout stand, I was boiling. Yet I said nothing to either the couple or the cashier. Nor did any of the people behind me who were just as miffed.

Why did we do that?

Why did I do that?

I knew people were breaking the rules, but I stood by silently and let them. And then I complained to myself about how rude they were.

And they were rude—very rude—and dishonest. But I was a coward. And to me, that was the greater sin.

Cowardice, in the name of politeness or patience, is probably more to blame for the ills of our society than the sins themselves, because cowardice lets the sin continue. Evil abounds when good people do nothing.

When good people who know the truth about life say nothing, millions of unborn children die.

When good people who know the truth about sexual relations say nothing, perverse behavior becomes the norm.

When good people who know the truth about salvation say nothing, other people go to hell.

If I won't speak out to stop the evil, I have no right to complain when the world goes the way of it.

Silence is not always golden.

Sometimes it's yellow.

I have often assented to sin by being silent, Father.
Forgive me.
From this moment on,
give me the courage of my convictions,
a heart for sinners,
and the boldness to speak the truth in love.

Likewise the Spirit also helpeth our infirmities:
for we know not what we should pray for as we ought:
but the Spirit itself maketh intercession for us
with groanings which cannot be uttered.
ROMANS 8:26

After watching the Summer Olympics,

my children were inspired. Suddenly, my living room was Olympic Stadium.

Thomas stood on his head.

Anna did a flying somersault and came within inches of breaking her neck and my chair.

Ben was the most devoted athlete. He jumped and tumbled. In the corner of the mat he struck a pose, with his head down and leg up. Then he threw himself sideways, landing on his bottom.

"Look, Mommy! Just like TV."

He did his trick again the same way.

"See? Just like TV."

He was so happy with his accomplishment, I couldn't tell him how much work it took to be "just like TV." Instead, I said, "That's good, Ben. Do it again."

And he did, again and again.

As he did, I saw myself.

When it comes to living the Christian life, I am so much like Ben. I think I'm doing it "just like Bible," when in reality, I'm far from it.

I read my Bible and pray. But sometimes I forget

what I read; sometimes I fall asleep when I pray.

I promise Him I'll remember that "a soft word turneth away wrath," but as soon as there is a squabble among children, I become a foghorn, which does nothing to abate their anger.

I pray for my neighbors to know Christ, but I've not even met them. How can I tell them of Jesus' love if I don't go out of my door to show them mine?

I take my children to church nearly every time the door is open. But sometimes on the way there, we bicker.

Sigh.

I'm no better than Ben. I am a child, playing at Christianity, falling far short of my high calling in Christ Jesus.

As Ben will not learn to stand on his hands without help, so I cannot live the Christian life without help. The Father knows this; He designed it that way. He gave me the very faith I needed to believe, and once I did, He gave me the Spirit to strengthen me and intercede on my behalf.

Like Ben, I have a long way to go until I'm doing it "just like Bible."

Like Ben, I will fall along the way, but remain cheerful.

Like Ben, I can get up again.

And in the Spirit, I will.

Lessons for a Supermom

Each day, I fall so short of Your high mark, Father.
While I am ashamed of my weaknesses,
I rejoice in the strength of the Holy Spirit who
seals, comforts, and protects me.
I'm so grateful for mercies that are new every morning
and for the Spirit who helps my infirmities.

Therefore thou art inexcusable,
O man, whosoever thou art that judgest:
for wherein thou judgest another,
thou condemnest thyself;
for thou that judgest doest the same things.
ROMANS 2:1

While writing a check at the grocery store, I asked the cashier to verify the amount.

When she did not answer immediately, I looked up. Her eyes were wide and her mouth agape as she stared into the next aisle.

Instinctively, I turned.

In the next aisle, fewer than six feet from her distracted mother, a preteen girl was standing atop a baby seat in a shopping cart. She was in a precarious position, teetering above a cement floor on an unstable, wheeled apparatus.

"Excuse me, Ma'am," I said. "Your daughter—"

When the mother looked up, she had that embarrassed, angry look we mothers get in those situations. She growled as politely as she could, and the daughter got down.

The cashier kept staring at the mother and children as they went through the line. I finished my business and left.

Had I been the cashier, I might have gawked more, too. But I'm a mother. I've walked in that mother's shoes.

My children have done all sorts of things they "knew better than" to do in public places. They've stood in carts, crawled on shelves, dropped (and broken) jars of food, run into traffic, and knocked over drinks in restaurants (and that's just for starters!).

Each time, I've been the embarrassed, ashamed mother. I've sensed the judgment of strangers and read their thoughts in the looks on their faces: "How could she let her child do that? Why wasn't she holding his hand? If she can't control them, she shouldn't have had children, especially not *that* many!"

I've known what it's like to feel an inch tall, to feel torn between running away or standing bravely and saying, "I'm not a rotten mother. I just haven't succeeded in teaching total obedience."

Having known unfair criticism, I try not to judge other mothers in similar circumstances, despite the strong temptation. (Why did the mother allow the kid in a baby seat in the first place?) Because I can never know the entire situation, I am an unworthy judge.

We are all unworthy judges. But we can all take comfort in the fact that our Ultimate Judge is holy, righteous, and omniscient.

And He is merciful. He sent Christ to take the punishment we deserve.

When Christ died for our sin, He also took away our shame.

Even the occasional shame of being with our kids in public.

. . .

Father, I'm so glad You protect my children from
the many stupid things they do that
I don't see "right under my nose."
Remind me of all these times when
I am tempted to judge another mother.
Help me not to criticize, but to comfort.
Let me be gracious, knowing You have given me grace.

There hath no temptation taken you but such as is common to man: but God is faithful, who will not suffer you to be tempted above that ye are able; but will with the temptation also make a way to escape, that ye may be able to bear it.

1 Corinthians 10:13

My sixteen year old was flustered.

"Why am I going through this? I bet no preachers have ever doubted the existence of God. I'm the only one."

"No temptation has taken you, but such as is common to man," I said.

"But the great men of faith wouldn't—"

"The great men of faith had clay feet, too. There's nothing new under the sun. You're not alone."

"But why would I—"

"Because such is common to man."

He went away shaking his head.

He wanted his trial to be unique, to be The Great Struggle of the Ages.

Isn't that just like a man? Or a woman?

So often I think that "nobody know de trouble I seen." I think I'm the only one who has ever encountered a particular situation, trial, or temptation. But Scripture says that just isn't so.

By the time the flood waters picked up the ark, mankind had already "been there, done that." After the seasons began, there really was "no new thing under the sun," until the Son became flesh and lived among us.

Do I doubt the Word of God? This is unbelief. Eve did the same.

Am I tempted to disobey the speed limit? This is rebellion against higher authority. It's Adam's original sin.

Do I get so angry I want to harm another physically? Cain did.

Mankind just keeps recycling experiences, because mankind never changes. Jesus "needed not that any should testify of man: for he knew what was in man" (John 2:25).

What is in man is a propensity to sin. Our common bend toward evil leads to our common temptations.

But thankfully, God provides the way of escape. Sometimes it's a literal way—a friend drives up at just the right time to keep you from walking through the "sleazy" section of town. But even then it involves the true way of escape, which is found in obedience to the Word of God.

When you get right down to it, God Himself is the way of escape. And our pride is the only thing that keeps us from safety. When I think, "I can handle this myself," it's a sure sign that I can't.

Our common trials require the strength of our uncommon God.

Only He can see us through.
Only He will.

. . .

Why do I have such a tendency to
succumb to temptation and crumble in crises?
I think I can handle the challenges of life without You.
Then I live like an atheist, not a child of God.
Only You are my very present help in trouble.
Thank You for not leaving me alone.

LOVING GOD
THROUGH LOVING OTHERS. . .

A man's love for a woman is to be as Christ's love for the church. If I am going to see God anywhere, I will see Him in my marriage and the marriages of those close to me.

I am my beloved's,
and his desire is toward me.
SONG OF SOLOMON 7:10

The pages from a school tablet
are brittle and brown,
but the story on them is lively and passionate:

The Romance of Girl and Boy
"The young man sat down before the table
at which he was writing a letter. No one
knew who he was writing to nor would anyone find out. . . .

"At last the letter was finished. He went
to his room and brought out a picture of a
beautiful girl. He kissed it once, twice,
three times, then looked to heaven and
prayed that some day not far off he might
make her his own, his own to love, to protect, and to keep. . . .

"In a few days he received an answer. . . .
He read the letter once, twice, then sat
down to answer it that day. He had never
seen her, but lived in hopes he would see her
some day. . . .

"The next letter he received told him
she was coming up that Sunday. He
kissed the letter and got her picture and

kissed it over and over. . . .

"At last the day came when she [came]. This young man was too bashful to go to her aunt's. His uncle went to her aunt's and brought her to this young man's home. His eyes shone with delight as he beheld her rosy cheeks, dark hair, sparkling eyes and ruby lips. He took her for a walk around the town. . ."

Many weeks later, the girl came for another visit and she was "more beautiful than before." They were together every night for two weeks. The day she went home, the young man rode along.

"That was a happy ride. . .for he had her in his arms all the time, but he was sad for he would not see her for some time. . . .

"(When they met [again] he put the shiny band around her dainty finger which meant she would be his sometime.) I guessed about the last part of it, but I hope it comes true."

The last part did come true.

My grandparents married in 1923. Their marriage survived the Great Depression and nearly fifty-six years of household trials.

My grandmother kept this story hidden in her

desk. She let me see it after my grandfather died; when she died, I asked my aunt for it.

While others got their furniture and jewelry, I got the real treasure.

I got their love.

. . .

I've been so blessed by my grandparents' legacy of love.
Let our love endure like theirs,
so I can pass the legacy to my grandchildren.

Likewise, ye husbands,
dwell with them according to knowledge.
1 PETER 3:7

In September 1997,
Rex Morgan finally married June Gale

in what was possibly the longest weekend in the history of the comics page, lasting from May until September.

When it was all over, Rex was in the kitchen cooking when June came home from school. Jane read the strip, then looked at me.

"Mom, did Rex Morgan marry June?"

"Yes," I said, "and it's about time."

"Why did he do that?" she said. "I thought they were best friends."

Answers bounced around my brain. "Well," I stammered, "sometimes people do marry their best friends."

But more often, they marry strangers. And it's a good thing, too.

If we had really known the nitty-gritty about our intended mates, fewer of us would have married. There would have been too many excuses not to.

Would I have married him had I known he snored liked a lawn mower? Or that he had been a nerd—and did not totally outgrow it?

Would he have married me if he had known I was a workaholic who was tied to a dead mother's apron strings?

In blissful ignorance, many of us tie the knot. Then we spend the next fifty years trying to figure out why.

But that's really the challenge of marriage. We make a commitment to another not knowing them or the future. Sometimes we get hurt, but as we persevere we do find joy. It may be as thrilling as when a comatose husband reaches for his wife's hand, or as mundane as when a wife stops squeezing the toothpaste in the middle.

The real joy and strength in marriage come not from knowing it all from the start, but from staying together once the truth is out.

One of these days, June will learn something new about Rex (he likes mackerel). And their marriage (and the kitchen odor) will be stronger than it was before.

. . .

Lord, let my husband learn to understand me,
and let me honor him even when I fail to comprehend him.
Let us grow closer to each other
as we both gain more knowledge of You.

For whom he did foreknow,
he also did predestinate to be conformed
to the image of his Son,
that he might be the firstborn among many brethren.
ROMANS 8:29

I stood at the back of the church listening as my then-roommate played her flute along with the piano. It was beautiful.

In fact, everything was beautiful. The day was gorgeous. The church was full of happy faces. I was thin and young and pretty.

Then the music changed. The sweet melodious flute phrases gave way to a heavy bass note followed by a bold chord. A Brahms march! Stately. Demanding.

The time had come.

I looked at my father, took a deep breath and smiled. We moved toward the door, then down the aisle.

With each step, I wondered if he knew how scared I was. What was I doing? Committing my life to a man I had known seven months?! Was I crazy?

Still, I kept walking, and kept smiling.

When I reached Michael, I was still shaking. But when I took his hand, I knew everything would be all right. Married life was going to be just perfect.

Perfect?!

On Day Two, he drove my new car into the hotel where we were staying.

During Month Three, I sat outside the Guam International Airport, my left leg in a cast to my knee, waiting for my beloved to pick me up and take me to our island paradise. When he finally arrived, he walked right past me. Later that same day, on our way to church, the rental car we were driving was rear-ended.

Perfect?

Sometime during Year One, we went to the beach one evening. During a romantic moment, I flirtatiously cast aside my glasses. And he sat on them.

Sometime during Year One, Year Two, and Years Three through Nineteen, I burned his supper. Usually the rice. Occasionally the beans. Frequently the garlic bread for the spaghetti. A few times, even the spaghetti sauce.

In Year Fourteen, I broke my leg and ankle while delivering newspapers with Son #1—forty minutes before Mike was to leave town for a month. (He didn't go.)

And in Years One through Nineteen, we actually raised our voices to each other.

Perfect?

There have been crises, misunderstandings, disappointments. But there have also been times of contentment, peace, and joy.

But all have worked together perfectly—according to God's plan—to make us both more like Christ.

No, married life hasn't been perfect.

But with God, it's still beautiful.

Sometimes I wonder why You put us together, Father.
We are at times so different. Yet through the differences,
You are making us more alike—
not like each other, but like Christ.
After so many years, there are still rough edges.
Keep sanding us down, Lord,
until only Your grain shines through.

Giving honour unto the wife,
as unto the weaker vessel.
1 PETER 3:7

The house was quiet—too quiet.

In the silent darkness, a mother alarm went off—The Paperboys! Had they gone back to bed? Why didn't I hear them?

I bolted out of bed and flew toward the black hallway—

BAM! A sharp pain exploded through my face and body.

"OWW!!!" I grabbed my face and fell backward. "WHO SHUT THE DOOR?"

The scream shocked Mike awake: "WHAT WAS THAT? WHAT'S WRONG?"

"I WALKED INTO THE DOOR!"

"HOW DID YOU WALK INTO THE THE DOOR? WERE YOUR EYES OPEN?"

(If they had been open years ago, this might not have happened.)

"Yes, my eyes were open. But it's dark—"

"You would have seen light down the hall."

"I'm sorry. I'm tired. I wasn't thinking," I sobbed. "I just wanted to make sure the boys were up. Why did you shut the door?"

"The boys were making too much noise."

My face felt numb and flat. I sensed blood. "Oh

great. My nose is bleeding. I think I broke it."

"Do I need to take you to the emergency room?"

"It can wait for office hours. I'll put ice on it. Go back to bed."

"Right. I'll just go back to sleep while you're in pain." He paused a moment. "What do they do if it's broken? Can they put your face in a cast?"

"No, they'll put my head in a sling."

We met the paperboys by the stairs. "What happened?! We heard a scream."

"Your mother ran into a door."

They wisely said nothing then, but their eyes were laughing as they followed us to the kitchen.

"You know, Mom," Matthew said, "if it didn't hurt, it would be funny."

Beneath the ice pack, the scene played out in my mind. I began to laugh. He was right—in a stupid sort of way, it was funny.

But, oh boy, did it ever hurt.

. . .

Oh, Father,
let me remember that the little aches and pains of life
are nothing when compared with the joys of eternity,
even when those I love are responsible for the hurts.

[Charity]. . .hopeth all things.
1 CORINTHIANS 13:7

The year was 1946.

He was twenty-six. A tall, handsome man in a uniform.

She was eighteen. Blond and petite and as pretty as a California girl ever gets.

And when the war was over, they, like millions of other couples, made tracks to the altar.

In a dozen years, they added five babies to the boom.

They were a typical fifties family. He worked; she stayed home. He made the money; she spent it.

They had their share of parenthood trials—childhood illnesses and emergencies, and paychecks that didn't always stretch between paydays. But they adapted and survived.

In the early sixties, she had a nervous breakdown.

"That was our hardest time," she said. "But Dad stayed with me and didn't give up, and he could have."

She and the marriage recovered.

In 1965, his job took them from California to Houston. She learned to dress western, talk with a drawl, and root for the Aggies.

She started working outside the home, doing jobs that were much like her household duties. She bossed teenagers at Dairy Queen, talked on the phone for Sears, then bossed big guys on the Sears loading dock.

The kids left home for college and marriage. The nest emptied, but the pictures on the television multiplied with each grandchild. So they bought a bigger TV.

In the eighties, his job took them to Venezuela. They learned to speak Spanish. She argued with cabdrivers. They returned to Houston in 1986; he retired a few years later.

Now it's 1996. He's still tall and handsome, but his step is slower and his hair is thinner. She's still petite and pretty and full of energy.

They are my in-laws, Glenn and Audrey Middlebrooke. Today, June 9, 1996, they are celebrating their fiftieth anniversary.

"We have had our disagreements at times," she admitted. "But our love has been stronger than the disagreements."

Theirs has been a life of ordinary wonders and mundane miracles.

A marriage made in heaven but forged on earth.

An example to follow.

. . .

Father, I am inspired by the example of my in-laws.
*Help me honor them by continuing the tradition of
a lasting marriage and a steadfast and enduring love.
Make us an example for our children to follow.*

And they shall be one flesh.
GENESIS 2:24

For years, Constance dreamed of marriage.
Like many of us, she wanted to be loved and to love.
But she made it through her twenties single. As each
year passed in her thirties, marriage seemed to be
more distant. Yet she kept hoping.

Her hope was fulfilled at age forty. She married a
widower, Harold, a man she had known many years.

They had a wonderful married life and were looking forward to retirement, so they could spend even
more time together.

But their dream did not go as planned.

In October 1995, a blood vessel burst in Harold's
brain. By the grace of God and thanks to Constance's
persistence, Harold walked out of the hospital less
than three months later, talking.

After being home a week, he suffered a massive
bleed. Through a series of miracles, he got to the hospital alive.

Harold is still alive. He is in a nursing home, in
what doctors call a "comatose" condition. But Harold
is no vegetable. Although he can't speak, he can open
his eyes and respond to simple commands.

In February 1999, I saw Harold for the first time
since he became sick. What I saw amazed and humbled me. It was not Harold, but rather his room and
his wife, that caught my attention.

Harold's room is decorated to the hilt. A heart here. A flower there. Their picture on the dresser. On every surface is a reminder of her love for him.

And Harold's wife, who was always thin, is now heavy. Because she had been by his side from the beginning, Constance had been eating institutional and fast food for more than four years. For most of that time, she also juggled a stressful job with daily visits.

Looking at Constance, I saw the true unity of marriage. And I understood the words of Christ: "Greater love hath no man than this, that a man lay down his life for his friends" (John 15:13). She has given her life for Harold's, completely; without regret.

Looking at them I also realized how shallow my love is for my normal, healthy husband. Too often I forget that marriage is indeed a blessing.

Not long ago, a nursing home administrator told Constance she was spending too much time with Harold and that she should "get a life."

Constance rejected the advice.

Because she already has a life—Harold's.

And until God's ready, she will not let it go.

. . .

I'm thankful for the man You've given me, Lord.
Help me love him with
an everlasting love that is ever patient,
ever hopeful, ever faithful.

And he put them on the shoulders of the ephod,
that they should be stones for a memorial
to the children of Israel;
as the LORD commanded Moses.
EXODUS 39:7

My friend Dixie has a butcher-block table.

This is not a butcher-block-veneer table or even one with a butcher-block top. It's a real butcher's chopping block—the kind that withstands meat cleavers—with legs. It's sturdy. Solid. Resilient.

Dixie and her husband, Harland, bought it for their first anniversary. It was the last such table made by the Traverse City (Michigan) Maple Company.

"We had to have help getting it home and into our tiny first home," Dixie said. "We stood with our arms around each other and contemplated where we would be and what we would be like when the glistening wood began to show signs of age."

That was in 1973.

Since then, the table has occupied the corner of a series of small kitchens, although Dixie still dreams it will someday be the focal point of a large one. There were times she wanted to get rid of it, but sweet memories stayed her hand. Around that table relationships deepened as family and friends kneaded dough, chopped vegetables, or shared goodies.

The table now bears the marks of four children,

eight cats, and nine kittens. It has a scratch here, a burn mark there. There's a perfectly round indentation on the side where Harland reattached a snap on the baby's overalls.

"This table is like our marriage," Dixie said. "It isn't shiny and new anymore. The wood is splintering in places.

"But I never see that when I look at it. I see the gorgeous chopping block that symbolized permanence and family to us as a young couple."

Like Dixie, I have a "chopping block," only mine's a rocker. We bought it to rock the first one.

I'm not sure Mike understood why I had to have a wooden rocker. But he loved me, so he bought it. To me, it symbolized the maternal tradition established by my foremothers. It was the place where I would nurture, train, and inspire my children.

The first one is in his teens. The rocker, scratched and dinged by the very ones it nurtured, creaks and groans. I can't sit in it safely because the rungs need to be glued.

Though I don't use it much, I'll keep that rocker, just as Dixie keeps her table.

How could we sell them?

They are dreams we can see.

Hopes we can hold.

Love we can touch.

Father, they may be only wood,
but these things are memorials of our married lives.
Though they remind me of the nicks and bruises of life,
they also remind me of the permanence of love,
especially Your love.

Charity suffereth long.
1 CORINTHIANS 13:4

A month after we got a dog in South Dakota,
Mike decided he wanted to work on Guam.

To comfort the children, he promised them that
the dog, Peaches, could go along. That meant extra expenses for us and four months of quarantine for Peaches.

No sooner was Peaches home from the kennel than
she discovered the truth about Guam's "killer" toads.

One night she snagged a toad during her walk.
Instantly, both she and her owners were foaming at
the mouth.

"Peaches got a toad!" they screamed. *"What are we
gonna do?"*

The dog started throwing up.

The kids started crying.

I called the veterinarian. She said, "Rinse out her
mouth." (Oh, no problem!)

Mike and I dragged the dog outside to the hose.
He held the leash while I locked Peaches in my legs
and started rinsing. She tried to get away. When it was
all over, I was soaked and wrapped in the leash.

I looked at Mike. "Was this included in 'I do'?"

Toad-tainted dogs must fall somewhere in the "for
worse" part, along with leaky water heaters, totaled
trucks, utility bills, and braces.

Had I known this, I might have been less eager to

walk the aisle. But I, like most brides, was ignorant of the fine print between "I take thee" and "till death do us part."

I suppose that's good. If I could have foreseen all that would happen, I would not have had the guts to utter one word, much less two.

Had I not said "I do," I might not have had four miscarriages.

Or eight beautiful children.

I might not have moved six times.

Or collected friends on Guam, in Colorado, New York, Maine, and South Dakota.

Saying "I do" is reckless. In those little words lurk happiness and heartache, blessing and bitterness, dreams and nightmares.

It's amazing to me that any individual dares to pledge a whole lifetime to another. I'm truly awed when I see a marriage that lasts that long, because there are times in all marriages when it's easy to wish you had stayed single.

Sometimes—like when I'm trying to nurse a baby, fix supper, and comfort a screaming toddler simultaneously—I wonder why I didn't keep quiet in 1981.

But I just had to say "I do."

And really, I'm glad I did.

Love is blind. Commitment sees.
I'm glad the love comes first and
You gradually open our eyes to reality.
I'm thankful You have walked with us
through our marriage, Father.
We cannot do it without You.

> *Thou art snared with*
> *the words of thy mouth.*
> PROVERBS 6:2

Truth be told, I never said, "I do."

Yes, I said it in essence, but not in fact.

I was one of those "free spirits" who insisted on writing my own vows. I was, after all, a writer. Surely I could come up with something more meaningful than the trite "for richer, for poorer" lines.

And I did, at least I thought I did. People complimented both of us on our vows.

But guess what?

Those were the days before ubiquitous videotapes, and someone forgot to turn on the cassette recorder. I've long ago lost the paper with those once-precious words. So if anyone, including Mike, asks what I pledged back then, I really cannot say.

Maybe those old lines are not so trite after all. Those who have said them can at least remember what they vowed to do.

The traditional vows are certainly pithy and all-encompassing. I can't think of any situations in marriage not covered by the "for better for worse, for richer for poorer, in sickness and in health" umbrella.

Perhaps that's why people don't like the old vows. There's nothing left out. If you write your own words, it's much easier to say, "Hey, I didn't promise to do that! I'm outta here!"

When traditional vows were the norm, society knew what was expected in marriage. That didn't keep all couples faithful to each other, but it did create a certain cultural accountability.

The old vows also set a high moral standard. When everyone vowed to be committed "till death do us part," divorces were less common. Modern marriage services often eliminate that phrase or replace it with a loop-hole: "as long as our love shall last."

Some might say the words really don't matter. They'd say I'm just as married having said "my own" vows as I would have been reciting traditional ones.

But am I? If I don't know what I agreed to, can I be sure I'm holding up my end of the bargain? And if his words were different from mine, did we really agree to the same marriage?

Words have meaning and consequences. They "snare" us.

When it comes to marriage vows, we'd all do well to be caught in the same trap.

Dear Father,
You have upheld us through this marriage
even though our vows were not in exact agreement.
Thank You for holding us together in the Spirit.
Our commitment to You has sustained
our commitment to each other,
even in the "for worse" times.

My son, keep thy father's commandment,
and forsake not the law of thy mother.
PROVERBS 6:20

My mother gave me two rules concerning marriage.

First she said, "You will never marry Tony." (Tony was of a different faith, and she had seen the frequent failure of such "mixed" marriages.) She also said, "Marry somebody smart; you don't want stupid children."

Wanting Mom's blessing upon my life, I took her words to heart. Every prospective husband was measured by her yardstick. When Mike—a Bible-believer with a degree from MIT—showed up, I didn't let him go.

Mom's advice was good as far as it went. Over the years, however, I've thought about what I'll add to it when I advise my children. I can think of one more rule: "If you want to marry him because you're in love with him, don't."

I'm sure they'll scratch their heads over this, but they will eventually understand. But probably not until the honeymoon is over.

Love, particularly as it is defined nowadays, is the worst reason to marry another. This love is some fuzzy state of being that one can fall into, and, apparently, out of. It's a selfish feeling that can rise and fall like the tide.

When modern couples pledge to be faithful "as long as we both shall love," the wedding might as well be adjourned to the divorce court, because that's where the marriage is headed.

Even biblical love, which seeks the good of the other, is not a good reason to marry. This love is an action that grows out of a self-sacrificial attitude. This love does things—it believes, hopes, rejoices, endures.

Successful marriages need this kind of love, but they are not built on it. Actions and attitudes can waver; they are not solid enough for a foundation.

The foundation is commitment. In performing the first wedding, God said the man "shall cleave unto his wife." Cleaving was mandatory; no "love" was required. No conditions applied. (He said nothing about her changing girth or his fluctuating state of employment.) The love— "two shall be one flesh"—came later.

In the beginning, marriage was a simple, lifelong commitment.

And it still is.

And when my children—boys or girls—are prepared to make that kind of commitment to another of like faith, they will get my blessing.

Because then they'll be ready to marry.

And to love.

Lessons for a Supermom

As my children reach the years when
they will search for a marriage partner,
make their hearts tender
and ears ready to listen to my advice.
Give me Your heart,
so I can advise them with Your wisdom.

For God giveth to a man that is good
in his sight wisdom, and knowledge, and joy.
ECCLESIASTES 2:26

While preparing the schoolroom,

I moved many toys. Blocks. Books. Skates. Snorkels.

And telescopes.

To make better use of space, I had to wrestle Mike's two telescopes out of the corner.

The smaller telescope, a six-inch reflector, is a long metal tube on a heavy stand. The legs form a Y and take up nine square feet of floor space. To move it, I had to hug the tube and grasp the main joint beneath. Then. . .ugh. . .lift!

Hug. Lift. Step. Drop. Hug. Lift. Step. Drop. Groan.

The other has a twelve-inch diameter and looks like a water heater. It takes up four square feet; it can be slid.

Hug. Slide. Push. Hug. Slide. Sigh.

Why must I have telescopes in my living area? Some women decorate in Early American. Others, in French Provincial. Still others, in Nouveau Attic.

But me? I decorate in Classic Astronomy.

I do so out of necessity. Telescopes are expensive. They can't be left in unheated Maine sheds or un-cooled Guam ones. So like the dog, they stay in the house. They're part of the family.

They're especially part of Mike.

Mike has been an amateur astronomer almost

forever. He started reading astronomy books at five; he got his first telescope at eight. He has drawings of planets dating from his teen years.

He has subscribed to *Sky and Telescope* magazine more than thirty years; he reads it cover to cover every month. That magazine collection has also moved around the world with us.

Mike knows the sky so well, he once spotted a small, unpublicized comet while on a mission to Wake Island. The other crew members didn't believe him until the paper reported the comet the next day.

Although he sometimes thinks I don't like his hobby (I don't relish getting up at 2 A.M. to look at anything), the truth is that I admire him for it. His love for astronomy has been a lifelong passion. It's his joy; his delight. I never want him to lose it.

As long as he lives, I will live with the telescopes. Should anything happen to him, I might sell the "water heater," but I'll never part with the other. It will always be a part of us.

Mike is also passionate about music.

I share my bedroom with a cello. . . .

. . .

My husband's interests have enriched my life.
I pray You will give him many strong years
so he can continue to enjoy
the passions You've given him.

And Ruth said, Intreat me not to leave thee, or to return from following after thee: for whither thou goest, I will go; and where thou lodgest, I will lodge: thy people shall be my people, and thy God my God.

RUTH 1:16

Several years ago, I began walking through widowhood.

Not my widowhood, thankfully. It was the widowhood of my dear friend, Twila. Her husband died of a neurological disease in 1987.

In the early months of widowhood, Twila wrote frequently. I was a good person to "dump" on because I wasn't "family" and I wasn't "there." I was a safe companion to share her journey.

At the beginning, her shock was in the reaction of others:

"The part that just blows my mind is the fact that even before [his] body was in the ground, the unattached males were coming up out of the ooze!" she wrote two weeks down the road.

Because the loss was so fresh, it was easy for her to put them off, and they eventually went away.

Other issues weren't quite as easy.

"I've been trying to figure out. . .what 'stage' I'm in—but it eludes me," she wrote at three months. "I just know I've never felt so strange (or 'estranged') in my life and it really is disconcerting. I still cannot get interested in anything! I don't feel 'led' to be despondent or depressed, especially, and I have no problem with getting up every morning and getting on with whatever duties or chores await.

"It's just that nothing matters! . . . It really is an awful feeling. Daisy and Maude [two widows] insist it will go away eventually and they'd better be right."

Things did improve, mainly because Twila faced the situation head-on. She dealt with the nitty-gritty issues (headstones, veterans' benefits) without complaint.

And rather than wallowing in grief, she acted upon it. After the funeral, she took off her wedding ring, because the marriage was over. But a few months later, she replaced it with a family ring made of stones representing four generations of family members. This, she said, was a "frivolity," but it gave her much joy.

A year down the road, Twila spoke at a bridal shower. She discussed the things many people think make a good marriage, and concluded that good marriages are those in which the husband and wife are committed not only to each other, but also to Christ.

These comments, more than the volume of letters I accumulated in the dozen years that followed, explained why Twila had a good widowhood.

Hers had been a good marriage.

Establish my marriage in You, Father.
Let me be obedient in this relationship now,
so I have no regrets should the time come when
I must walk the road alone again.

And the Lord God formed man
of the dust of the ground,
and breathed into his nostrils the breath of life;
and man became a living soul.

GENESIS 2:7

As a mother of boys, I sometimes worry.

I worry that they'll never learn to wear shoes and socks simultaneously. I fret that they will always think "clean up your room" means "fill up your closet." I live in horror that they will go to college and wear the same shirt the whole semester.

But most of all, because my sons spend so much time with me, I sometimes fear they will not grow up fully masculine. How can I be sure that they will not be overly influenced by my emotional approach to life? Given a situation, will they know how to react as men?

I wonder. And I watch. Here's what I've seen:

— They already act like men. The littlest man-child thinks I exist to wait on him hand and foot. When he doesn't get his way, he screams and throws fits.

— They won't do a tedious job (strip wallpaper) unless they can rescue me from it. ("Let me do that for you, Mom.")

— They cannot tell when a trash can is full. And they don't know it's okay to empty it without being told.

— They think like men: John asked where couples should go on a honeymoon.

"Some place your wife will enjoy," I said.

"I know!" Matthew said. "Fishing!"

— They think the bathroom is the British Museum Reading Room. I've got one who even takes his math book in with him!

While being instructed on the subtleties of laundry, Matthew complained, "Why does the washer turn everything inside out?" (It takes a Y chromosome to think like that!)

— They talk like men: John comes in the door like Jackie Gleason: *"Mommy, I'm hoommme!"*

When I burned a huge pot of beans, Charles coughed melodramatically. "Next time, why don't you try not to burn them?" (Next time, I'll serve them scorched.)

I don't have to worry. Maleness runs deep. Boys will be men.

For better or for worse.

Dear Father,
grant me wisdom to teach my sons
that though they must think like men,
they must learn to think about the needs
of the women around them.
Help me show them an example of
a godly woman so they will be able to
choose godly wives.

So God created man in his own image,
in the image of God created he him;
male and female created he them.
GENESIS 1:27

I was discussing a problem with my two oldest.

The problem was the kids' bathroom, which they are supposed to keep clean.

It's a difficult chore. The toilet doesn't flush well, so it doesn't stay clean very long. And then we have that other problem, common to households with boys.

"Somebody's missing," I said, "and he's not cleaning up after himself."

"I clean up!" one of them protested. "It is probably Ben."

"It doesn't matter who it is. I don't know how you can miss."

"We have to miss," John said, "it's our mentality."

"Exactly right. It's your MEN-tality. You're little men. . . ."

These little men of mine have been showing their true nature lately. I no longer lose sleep worrying about their masculinity. They will be men. They can't help it.

When the Bible says, "Male and female created he them," it's definitely not joking. God made males and females. He created each separately. He meant for us to be different.

Guys do have a certain MEN-tality. They just can't think like women do, even when they try. Some things just don't register with guys.

For example, don't expect the fudge icing to turn out if you give him a recipe that requires "an inch of sugar in the bottom of a pan and enough milk to make it 'thin but not runny.' " Instead of icing, you'll get a lecture about the ridiculousness of the recipe.

Don't expect to get the right panty-liners even when you give him the brand name, size, and style. He may have advanced degrees, but chances are he'll come home with the wrong pads. The only pads men understand are brake pads, legal pads, and shoulder pads (the football kind).

It's an XY phenoMENon. As my boys get older, they naturally indulge in male behavior. They read the sports pages and watch the Superbowl.

When it comes to communication, they show male-pattern deafness. If it's a topic they like, they listen attentively and speak like scholars. But if not, it's best to save my spit.

For example, one is hooked on radios and computers. He understands words as transmitter, transceiver, megahertz, and midis. But say, "Get your shoes off the couch," and he'll say: "Shoes? Couch?"

How typically male!

And to think I have to go through this five times!

Will I survive?
I'll MANage.

. . .

Father, these little men You've given me are a challenge,
it's true. Let me train them to honor and respect women.
Help me appreciate their maleness
and teach them to possess it in wisdom.

*Husbands, love your wives,
even as Christ also loved the church,
and gave himself for it.*
EPHESIANS 5:25

A sportswriter I know once wrote a column explaining how simple men are.

Inspired by this, I wanted to write an essay explaining how simple women are.

But I couldn't. Because women are not simple.

Just ask Mike. After nineteen years, he still hasn't figured me out.

Say, for example, he comes home to find me crying. To his simple cause-and-effect mind, something must have caused the crying, so he reacts accordingly:

"What's wrong?"

"Nothinggggg," I'll wail.

"Then why are you crying?"

"I don't knowwwwww."

"Why don't you stop?"

"Because I feel like crying!"

He'll walk away shaking his head, muttering.

I also make him mutter at vacation time. While he leisurely packs his one suitcase, I clean the house, wash every piece of dirty laundry, pack for at least five kids and myself, and make sure all of them are in clean underwear (in case we have an accident).

Then I stuff my tote bag with unread magazines

and newsletters, receipts, and a few notebooks. The first hundred miles, I post receipts and tally food expenditures.

"Ah," he'll say, "we're on vacation."

That's what he thinks. I'm still trying to get caught up and organized so I can relax. My house and family are extensions of me—and if they're not in order, I'm not in order.

And then there are times when I'm stressed out over a problem:

"I've got to take two to piano lessons from 2:00 to 3:00, get two at school at 3:00 and be downtown for an appointment by 3:15. This is crazy!"

"So why don't you have the boys walk home?" he'll say calmly.

Idiot! I knew that. I didn't want him to solve my problem. I just wanted him to feel my pain.

Sometimes I wish I could be less complicated, but it's not in my nature.

And that's not my fault. We women have been complicated since creation.

God made Adam simply, from "the dust of the earth." But He made Eve from Adam's rib, a more complicated process.

We are wonderfully, annoyingly complex by design. We weren't meant to be figured out. We were meant to be loved.

It's as simple as that.

I know I annoy him, sometimes, Father,
because I look at life so differently.
Give him the wisdom to understand me
and the patience to endure.

And the LORD God said,
It is not good that the man should be alone;
I will make him an help meet for him.
GENESIS 2:18

For his ninth birthday,
Charles (the Boy Wonder)

got a game from his grandparents called "Rush Hour." The object of the puzzle game is to free your car from rush-hour congestion. This is done by moving plastic vehicles up and down files and back and forth on rows.

Charles likes mind teasers, so he does well with the game. And he enjoys showing off his intellect at the expense of his younger siblings.

One night I wanted something different to do, so I borrowed the game after Charles went to bed. I had hoped for a quiet challenge. Instead, I had an audience.

Matthew peered over my shoulder like a chauvinistic vulture.

"You know, Mom," he said smugly, "this is where males have an advantage."

"Oh, really?"

"Really. I read about it in *Reader's Digest.*"

I ignored him and moved a car. Meanwhile, my Dearly Beloved came to my rescue.

"Your mother is smarter than the average female," his father said chivalrously. He wandered toward the table and leaned over my other shoulder. "It's obvious—you're going to have to move the truck all the way down."

"Go away!"

"You're right, Matthew," his dad whispered as he left. "Males do have an advantage."

I ignored them both and solved the puzzle before Matthew did.

"Looks like we need a few more male minds over here," I said.

Matthew and I tried a more difficult puzzle, and I again solved it first. He decided it was bedtime and excused himself.

Male minds need more sleep, you know.

Male minds. Honestly!

Sure, they might—*might*—be more naturally inclined to mathematics, logic, and science, but so what? What good is the Pythagorean theorem when the rice is boiling over, the dinner guests are due in five minutes, and the baby needs changing?

Male minds are more solution-oriented. They like the facts, not the emotional details. And when we give them an emotional problem, they want to solve it like a math problem, even if we don't want a solution. Is this really "smart"?

And if male brains are so superior, why don't they understand women? We're expected to know what makes them tick. We are understanding and empathetic. But they just look at us and scratch their heads.

No, male minds are not better, just different.
But do give them credit.
They are at least smart enough to marry female ones.

. . .

Having made us in Your image, Father,
You've given us creative and thoughtful minds.
Let me be wise enough to appreciate and love
the differences between his brain and mine.

[Teach the young women. . .]
to be discreet, chaste, keepers at home,
good, obedient to their own husbands,
that the word of God be not blasphemed.
TITUS 2:5

"Obedient to their own husbands."

What!? Me?! Obey him?!

Lord, You're kidding, right?

How can I obey him?

He makes mistakes.

He doesn't understand me.

Why, he's a man, and sometimes men just don't get it.

And Paul was writing in the first century. It was different then. Different culture. Different aspirations.

Surely God will make allowances in our modern world. Lots of women have to work outside the home and must obey men other than their husbands. And besides, women are more intelligent and independent now.

I know how to make my own decisions. Isn't it right that I should?

"Obedient to their own husbands."

Obedient?

To subject myself.

To submit to another's control.

To yield to another's admonition or advice.

The word in Scripture is a Greek military term

meaning "to arrange [the troops]. . .under the command of a leader." In non-military use, it was a "voluntary attitude of giving in, cooperating, assuming responsibility, and carrying a burden."

Obedience is an attitude that is expressed in an action. So is love. In marriage, obedience is love.

As I obey my own husband, I put myself under the leader God has established in the home. When I do this, I cooperate with Him in carrying the responsibility and burden of the family as He has designed.

That's why I should obey.

Not to make my husband feel good about himself.

Not because he's bigger or smarter or stronger than I.

But because I honor God and His Word if I follow His design.

Me? Obey him?

To obey Him, I must.

. . .

Sometimes I chafe under
the authority of my husband,
but I know it's my own fault—
it's my own stubborn heart.
I want to honor Your Word;
I want to honor my husband.
Give me the determination to obey.

GLORIFYING
GOD IN THE TRENCHES. . .

*Being a mother has taught me how much I
need the Lord, how much I need to rely upon
the Holy Spirit. It has taught me the real test
of faith is not on the mountain, it's in the
trenches.*

For God is not the author of confusion,
but of peace.
1 CORINTHIANS 14:33

Some days, I'm not a mother.
I'm a crisis manager.

Instead of purposefully guiding little lives, I often find myself a step behind, beset by the constant need to resolve little crises.

On any given day, there are property disputes ("I had it first! Make him give it back!"), freak accidents ("I didn't trip him. He fell over my leg."), equipment failures ("Mom! Something's wrong with the washer!").

There are broken toys, skinned knees; system errors, missing shoes; a fussy baby, a lonely teenager.

I didn't picture motherhood this way. I saw it as a warm fireplace with "Home Sweet Home" over the mantel. I envisioned a wise mother, leading her dear children with the confidence of General Patton and the compassion of Florence Nightingale.

Reality's not quite the same. It's more like a messy kitchen with a plastic bowl melting on a burner. It's a frenzied mother wondering what's for dinner, wishing bedtime were at 4 P.M.

Is it this way for every mother, or just for me?

One typical day, I was to be at the mall around 12:30 P.M. to meet some friends.

At 12:29, a pitcher of orange juice exploded in

the kitchen. I couldn't mop it up—the bucket was missing. While they looked for the bucket, boots and mittens vanished.

At 12:45, the kitchen was clean and the feet shod. "I haven't eaten yet," one whined. I tossed him some leftover pizza.

At 12:53, the snowsuited baby needed changing.

Finally at 1:07, I got in the car, muttering. Why were we doing this?

Oh yes. We were going to relax with friends. I hoped I hadn't missed them.

Upon arriving, I apologized. "Sorry I'm late."

"I just got here," one said.

Another mom showed up even later, stressed and worn, feeling unmotherly.

I looked at them and smiled to myself. I was not alone.

As mothers, we all live the same crazy lives.

Just in different houses.

. . .

Lord, I know You are not the author of confusion.
I ask for Your Holy Spirit to help me set my house in order.
And if peace can't reign in my house,
at least let it reign in my heart,
because I know that You are ever with me.

Lo, children are an heritage of the LORD:
and the fruit of the womb is his reward.
PSALM 127:3

1996

Now is the summer of my discontent—of puffy hands, legs as fat as coffee cans, and feet so full of fluid they squish.

It's summers like this that sometimes make me wish that I believed in planned pregnancies.

If I did, I certainly would not have planned to be this pregnant this summer. Last fall, I knew we had to drive to Texas in June. And no one in her right mind would want to be six months pregnant for a 2,600-mile trip in a van with no air conditioning.

No one in her right mind would plan to get pregnant after losing twenty-five pounds, returning her to a weight she hadn't seen in fifteen years.

And I don't suppose most women would plan a baby when they're breathing hard on forty and already have six children.

That's the problem with planned pregnancies. If we could totally control when children arrived, fewer would. (Since 1973, millions of babies have not come because their mothers wanted control.) Often "planned" pregnancy means "banned" pregnancy.

Babies rarely arrive when it's convenient, and never when it's perfect. Four of mine were born within five months of major moves. Not good timing. If I had chosen their birthdays they would have come earlier—or later—or maybe not at all.

That last possibility is frightening.

What if for the sake of my convenience, any one of these ill-timed, food-inhaling, asthmatic children had never been born? There would be more money, newer cars, and better furniture, but there'd be less laughter, fewer challenges, and fewer hugs. Each one has so much potential, so much promise. Without any one of them, I—and the world—would be so much poorer.

Children are a heritage of the Lord, and the fruit of the womb is His reward.

It's presumptuous to tell God when He can give rewards.

So I'll endure surprise pregnancies.

And long, hot summers.

. . .

*Father, I love all the surprise blessings You've sent.
How is it I am worthy of such rewards from You?
You are so good to me.
Let me be a good steward of these little lives,
remembering always that they are a trust from You.*

A woman when she is in travail hath sorrow,
because her hour is come:
but as soon as she is delivered of the child,
she remembereth no more the anguish,
for joy that a man is born into the world.
JOHN 16:21

Our five-year-old Timekeeper should have been pleased.

Baby Gus came on the due date.

But the Timekeeper wasn't totally happy when he met Gus.

"I wanted to see him be born," he fussed.

Although it was possible, it just wasn't practical. Besides, watching a birth is like seeing an iceberg. It's a great sight, but you witness only a small part of the truth.

Bearing children is more than just giving birth. Those who have done it, and we who are in the midst of it, know that children are borne for years.

We carry them along first in the womb, then in the arms. After they start walking, we carry them through the trials of growing up—lifting them up, holding them back, and gradually pushing them out into their own lives.

And while the pangs of labor are truly great, the pains of watching them stumble and fall later in life are harder and more lasting for mothers. One saintly mother I know ached for years as she watched her wayward son. He's back now, and she is rejoicing, but she will remember the heartache until she dies.

Despite the physical pain, the birth is the easiest part of the process.

Our latest birth was on August 27, 1996. Benjamin Bruce Middlebrooke was greeted not by his siblings, but by an ever increasing cast of medical personnel. Still, they welcomed him as his father and I did, with relief, gladness, and awe.

When the brothers and sisters did meet him three hours later they were thrilled, although three of them were slightly disappointed they had not witnessed the birth.

I doubt they would have understood it all.

They would have seen the pain and been amazed at the result. But they could not have known that my heart bore Benjamin more than my body did.

I bore my new son with commitment and humor, in love and pain.

And thus will I bear him for years to come.

Gracious Father, how joyful I am that
You have blessed me with another child.
Equip me for the task that lies ahead.
Let me carry and lead him through life with
wisdom, faith, and good humor.
And let me never forget You
did not intend for me to do this job alone.
I'm grateful You're walking beside me all the way.

Redeeming the time,
because the days are evil.
EPHESIANS 5:16

I have other things to do.

Three loads of wash await folding, the kitchen floor begs for mopping, and paper-route paperwork needs completing. Inside my brain, random phrases bounce like loose basketballs as I think about a writing deadline.

So much stuff—too much to get finished before bedtime.

But here I am, with a baby on my lap, going round and round and up and down on a carousel. Behind me, my six year old lectures his younger brother and sister about merry-go-rounds and carousels, about horse tails and whatever else captures his fleeting fancy.

Their giggles swirl with the tinny music. Like bubbles in the wind, they float around and over me. POP! Soon another laugh dances about me.

The smiles don't stop with the carousel. The kids get off the ride with new energy, eager to explore.

"Let's go to the castle!"

The boys take off running while I follow with the stroller duo, bemused. They have been to this park countless times, but to them it is new again. After all, it is a new day.

I watch them wistfully. Oh, to have the eyes of a child to see the world fresh each day! To have a child's mind that neither lingers on the past nor frets about the future. To live as children live—in the here and now.

To children, life is "now." And they are right. Life is now. We are promised nothing beyond this moment. Marriage and motherhood—and childhood—are not forever, but for now. Yet if we miss them now, we will have missed them forever.

They run to the playground near the mill.

"Mommy! Watch me!"

"Mommy! Push me!"

I lift my preschooler into the swing and give a push.

"I'm fwinging!" she laughs. "Higher!"

I give another push. And another.

Yes, I have other things to do.

But none better.

. . .

The moments of our lives—
the joyful and the sad—
are all precious, Lord.
Let me not squander them in vain pursuits,
but let me invest them in my children, my husband,
and the people You bring into my life.

Chasten thy son while there is hope,
and let not thy soul spare for his crying.
PROVERBS 19:18

I didn't give birth to children.

I gave birth to American Express Cards. And I don't leave home without them.

Leaving my house alone is like escaping from Alcatraz—almost impossible.

To get away during daylight, I must make a plan: Get the little ones napping, the middle ones busy and the baby-sitters (big brothers and Dad) properly instructed.

Then I create a diversion: "Go see if Anna's asleep yet." "Where are your shoes? Go get your shoes."

When all is clear, I make a dash out the back door. In a move worthy of a B western, I jump in the van, turn the key, buckle the belt, floor it, and I'm—

Stopped by a kid leaning out the door, yelling and whining: *"Mommy? Where are you going? I want to come!"*

"Oh, all right. Get in."

Sometimes giving in is more expedient than going alone. Besides, when I do go alone, I'm like a prisoner on the lam—guilty and pursued. Dogged by thoughts of weepy children, I hurry. Then I inevitably forget something and must go back later, with children.

To avoid the stress, I often shop after they drop for the day. It's easier than saying "no" or trying to explain.

A guy like John Rosemond, the syndicated columnist and child psychologist, would be appalled. "You owe them no explanation," he'd advise. "Leave. If they cry, let them. They'll get over it."

I agree—in my head. But sometimes I get mush-brained and softhearted. And what does it matter if a kid gets his way once? Next time, I'll do it right. Maybe.

One recent day, everything was perfect. Little ones, napping; middle ones, at a friend's house; baby-sitters alert. I sauntered to the van, opened the door, and—

Whoosh! A light brown streak whizzed by my skirt.

When I got in, our new dog was already in the passenger's seat.

She looked at me with big brown eyes and whined.

I turned the key and sighed.

At least I didn't try to explain.

. . .

*Father, doing what is right for my children
is sometimes difficult for me.
I know I must discipline them;
I must teach them that they have a place,
and it is not always with me.
Give me the fortitude to follow through,
knowing discipline will eventually yield
the peaceable fruit of righteousness.*

Those that be planted in the house of the LORD
shall flourish in the courts of our God.
They shall still bring forth fruit in old age.
PSALM 92:13–14

In the fall of 1996,

a sixty-three-year-old woman gave birth in California.

Sixteen years after being told she would never have children, Arceli Keh held her beautiful daughter, Cynthia, and smiled.

It was a miracle—until May 1997, when the world found out about it.

Within days, Mrs. Keh went from Miracle Mom to Criminal Mom. She was too old to have a baby! She had lied about her age! It was scandalous!

Journalists and ethicists attacked Mrs. Keh, insulting her intelligence and sanity. A few bleeding hearts ached because Cynthia's parents might not be at her graduation.

One columnist haughtily concluded the Kehs were "selfish" because they had risked leaving their daughter an orphan "just so they could feel young again."

What nonsense!

The Kehs' story is not one of selfishness, but of love and sacrifice. Mrs. Keh has a mother's heart—it was her deepest desire to nurture a child of her own. She kept praying for a baby even though it seemed impossible.

She and her husband, Isagani, a factory worker,

scrimped to save the thousands needed for the in vitro fertilization. The first implantations failed. During her pregnancy, she had diabetes. Later, she lost her amniotic fluid. And to top it off, she delivered by Caesarean. (All this just to feel young? I don't think so.)

The Kehs were an ordinary couple who had an ordinary desire to be parents, even though they were "old." God blessed that desire and gave them a baby. Why was that wrong? Why was it worthy of vilification by the media?

It's a symptom of our mixed-up culture. We wink at infidelity; we call sinful behaviors "diseases," and pornography "art." And then when something wonderful happens—an old woman gives life to a child—we call it "crazy."

Giving life is not crazy.

And some day—even if she stands alone at graduation—Cynthia will understand and appreciate that.

Even if no one else does.

. . .

Father, let me not criticize the choices and decisions made by others, even if they seem wrong or unusual to me. Children are a blessing. Thank You for enabling us women to give birth. It is an awesome calling to be a mother, to be used by You to carry on the race and continue Your plan on earth.

She looketh well to the ways of her household,
and eateth not the bread of idleness.
PROVERBS 31:27

The soft, black earth yielded up
the tiny plant without resistance.

I threw it aside. One more weed for the pile.

I tossed another and began to wonder: Why bother? If I spent all day and pulled up every last offender, there would be new weeds tomorrow. The job would be undone.

I sighed resignedly. It was just another kind of Mother Work. And a mother's work gets all undone.

I clean the floor and the first feet in the door are mud covered.

I make a bed and immediately a little person jumps on it.

I dress the baby and he spits up on himself within minutes.

I tell them to put their things away today, and tell them again tomorrow.

It's a great frustration, this futility of homemaking. On any given day, many things I do will have to be done again. Sometimes I wonder why I bother. I feel unproductive and unappreciated.

It would be so nice if just once they all would wipe their feet before coming into the house. Or if they all said "thank you" after a meal. (Applause might be nice, but that's pushing it.)

Once while sharing these frustrations with my Colorado mom, she readjusted my perspective.

"This is the busiest and most tiring time of your life," she said knowingly. "But your reward will come. Later. When you're a grandmother." (I should live so long.)

I know she is right. But sometimes—like when the baby christens my dry-clean-only dress with his breakfast—it's difficult to see the big picture and to realize that the little acts of motherhood are not really futile. Each task we do, even if it gets undone and must be repeated, moves us closer to the goal of adding a healthy, independent adult to society.

Someday the Mother Work will stay done.

They will be grown and gone. And the house will be clean.

And I'll be wishing I could do it all again.

. . .

Father, sometimes the mother stuff
gets tedious and repetitious.
Let me do it all to Your glory,
with resolve and good cheer.
This is my task. Let it also be my joy.

He shall fly away as a dream,
and shall not be found.
JOB 20:8

The house is very quiet.

Three children are napping upstairs; the husband is fixing lunch in the kitchen; the dog is curled up in the living room; and I'm writing in the office.

Beyond this, the house is empty. The other four children are at church camp.

I'm writing this on Day Four of my Temporary Emptying Nest Status. I am unsettled.

In the last four days, household stress has been noticeably reduced. And it's been fun to relax and play with the youngest ones.

But for every advantage of having fewer children home, there is a drawback:

— There are fewer dishes to wash. But I have to wash them—the dishwashers are gone.
— The bread is lasting longer. But the bananas are getting overripe.
— The paperboys aren't waking me up at five. But the alarm clock is—this week, I am the paperboy.
— I can work without interruption, so I have no excuse not to.
— The one that yells to be heard is now talking

more quietly, but she doesn't stop.
— When we go out, it's easier to keep track of
    the mob, but I find myself constantly think-
    ing, "I'm missing someone."

I am that someone.

I don't feel complete without all my children.
When just one is gone, I am not the same.

Without my seven year old's constant jokes or my
preteen's constant problems, my brain gets mushy.
Without the enigma, the socialite, the unassuming
one, the sassy one, or the little giggler, my life gets too
easy and predictable.

So much of who I am now is what I've become
because of them. Their lives are such a part of mine,
it's difficult to recall my life without them. Haven't I
always had them forever?

No, I haven't.

Nor can I keep them forever. But for now, I don't
like to let them go. Even if it's only for a week of camp.

While I was making lunch for the non-campers,
Anna came to talk.

"Mom," she said, "you only have three kids now."

"How did that happen?"

"The other four are at camp," she reported.

"Well, what am I going to do with the rest of you?"

"You're going to keep us until the rest of the guys
come back."

Until they come back, yes.
And for as long as I can.

. . .

Lord they're growing up so fast.
The day is almost past when their father
and I have the greatest influence in their lives.
Let me be a consistent and godly example—
so they will know how to respond as adults.
Let me not be afraid to let them go.
They were born for that. And so was I.

She perceiveth that her merchandise is good:
her candle goeth not out by night.
PROVERBS 31:18

Remember "Supermom," the mother who maintained a full-time job,

cared for her family, and kept her house clean—all in the same day?

She never existed. She was a media creation.

Several years ago, however, I discovered the real Supermom. And she lives within!

I remember the day she surfaced.

Life with the children had been particularly draining. In late afternoon, I plopped on the ugly couch. My hand fell beneath the cushion and hit a strange object—a petrified banana peel!

"That's it!" an inner voice screamed. *"You will get this house in order!"*

With that Supermom moved in.

Supermom is organized, fastidious, energetic, neurotic. She is faster than a runny nose, more powerful than a smelly diaper, able to leap Lego buildings in a single bound.

At first, living with her was difficult. She's a nag and a perfectionist: "Clean the refrigerator—the leftovers are walking." "There's a streak on the window—do it again."

I pity the children when Supermom is about. There

is no time for interruptions, no excuse for muddy shoes. And forget giggling—Supermom does not laugh.

Gradually, I've adapted. When there's lots of work and little time, she's terrific. She can make breakfast, do wash, and nurse a baby simultaneously. She's better than a maid—and a lot cheaper.

Supermom has disciplined me to keep the house reasonably clean and organized. And I appreciate her sense of duty.

But sometimes, she bugs me. She doesn't know the meaning of "rest." No job is done well enough to suit her. There's always something else that needs to be done.

I am tired of her constant grind. Life is more than housework. I want to live beyond her voice that tells me what I must do.

One of these days, she's outta here. Maybe I'll send her to a friend who needs her. Maybe I'll shoot her.

But not until she strips the dining room wallpaper and gets my office organized.

. . .

Lord, I know I am to be diligent in all I do.
Remind me that I don't need to do everything.
Show me Your will.
Give me the good sense to
live according to Your priorities.

Visiting the iniquity of the fathers
upon the children,
and upon the children's children,
unto the third and to the fourth generation.
EXODUS 34:7

The experts say
it is unwise to threaten children.

But every mother does it.

Motherly threats and curses help us cope. It is not so much that we levy a threat on a child to harm him. Rather, we say rash things to blow off steam, and maybe—if we're lucky—silence the child for a moment.

My mother had the usual arsenal of threats:

"Do that, and you'll put your eye out."

"Someday your face will freeze like that."

"Keep that up, and you'll lose your happy home."

We knew she never meant them. And we knew they never came true.

Except for one.

I don't remember what I was doing that day, but it must have been bad. I must have really been pushing her. When her eyes narrowed and her jaw tightened, I should have known it was too late.

She looked at me with fiery eyes and let me have it: "May you have a child just like you."

So far, I have six who are "just like me."

According to her, I was a "pest of the devil." I've

got two like that.

I was moody (got one), stubborn (got three), quietly defiant (got two), asthmatic (got five), and had a short temper (got one of those, and unfortunately he got a double dose because my mother-in-law uttered the curse, too).

This curse can't fail because when we reproduce, we reproduce more than bodies. We reproduce our attitudes and values in our children. For better or worse, they will be like we are.

One day, the stubborn, asthmatic, short-tempered one was nagging me with his latest idea to spend my money. He would not stop. He pushed me too far.

My eyes narrowed, and my jaw tightened: "May you have a child just like you!"

He stiffened and paled.

I know, it was cruel.

But he had it coming.

. . .

Father, forgive me.
I know it is not right to "curse" anyone,
especially my children.
I do pray for this one who is so like me.
When You see fit to bless him with another like himself,
help him love that little one patiently.
And help me do the same now.

But we were gentle among you,
even as a nurse cherisheth her children.
1 Thessalonians 2:7

The house is a trash heap.

The couch sprawls across the floor like a sloppy teenager. The slipcover is slipping; books and magazines cover the cushions.

An undressed doll naps on the carpet. A dress for another doll lays behind a chair.

In the baby corner, blankets are everywhere—on the antique trunk, on the floor, in the carriage.

And that's just the living room! The dining room is littered with newspapers. The kitchen floor is prematurely gray (it's supposed to be white!).

All around me the house cries for attention. Windows long for curtains. Walls beg for new paper. The carpet aches for the Rug Doctor.

It's enough to make my perfectionistic palms sweat.

But I do nothing about it. I just sit in my rocking chair, nursing the baby.

While the baby thrives, the housework languishes. Dishes sit in the sink between meals. Wash that used to take one day to finish takes three. With all the interruptions, meals that took fifteen minutes now take an hour.

High priority chores get done of necessity, often

after bedtime; some things are done haphazardly by my helpers; some jobs aren't done at all.

From my rocking vantage point I see the mess. But I also see the mess-makers.

That little blond doll-dropper slept contentedly in my arms just two years ago. Five years ago, I prayed for that kid with the muddy shoes to walk. And the young man reading the latest newspaper poll used to sit on my lap to read Dr. Seuss.

All too soon, this little one won't want to be babied. He'll be as independent as the rest of them. Faster than I can imagine, he'll be grown and gone. Then my nest will be empty—and clean.

His tummy is full now. I could get back to work. I glance at the couch. I stare at him.

Then I close my eyes and keep on rocking.

. . .

Father, I'm so grateful for the ability to nurse my children;
for those precious times of nurturing.
Let me never take them for granted,
and let me not give them up for the sake of a career or things.
If I am tempted to want "freedom,"
remind me that the greatest freedom is
always within the boundaries You have set.

And thou shalt teach them diligently
unto thy children,
and shalt talk of them when
thou sittest in thine house,
and when thou walkest by the way,
and when thou liest down,
and when thou risest up.
DEUTERONOMY 6:7

It was an unusual sight for a Sunday morning in November.

A pristine blanket of snow covered the world. It was all white—the sidewalk, street, shrubs, trash cans—everything. Everything except that body on my front yard.

The body on my front yard?!

A lifeless form wrapped in nylon and down lay on the snow, a canvas newspaper bag by its side. I watched for movement, but saw none.

I opened the door and quizzically called to my paper carrier: "Angie? Are you all right?"

"Ohhh!" The body groaned and turned. It was my carrier's mother! She was well, but obviously tired. "I was just waiting for Angie."

"What a day to be out delivering papers," I said. "When I saw the snow, I was so thankful we no longer have a paper route."

"I was cursing the paper route today," she said.

I understood. It was only a few minutes after seven,

but she had already been up two hours. Already she had driven through unplowed streets to drop off paper bundles for another daughter. Already she had trudged through unshoveled snow to deliver dozens of papers.

"My thighs are killing me," she said. "I don't need a Stairmaster today."

I know my carrier's mom was not alone. Throughout the area that morning, parents were slogging through the mess, helping their young carriers with their jobs. Thighs and backs ached all day for the sake of a child's success.

But it's not just carrier parents, and it's not just on snowy days. Every day parents ache for their child's success in school, in jobs, in sports, in music. Wherever his greatness lies, we want him to find it. And we're willing to drive to practices, make costumes, raise money, and dodge lightning bolts to help.

Sometimes it's a pain. But as we work together with them, they see our diligence; they learn responsibility.

Angie finally caught up. She pulled her mother from the snow.

And then they trudged on.

Together.

Father, as I work with my children,
let me teach them of You and what You value—
diligence, honesty, and integrity.
And please, Father, give me the grace to
sometimes let go of my desires
so they can achieve their goals.

Therefore shall a man leave
his father and his mother. . . .
GENESIS 2:24

1996

Matthew and Sally had been buddies since she had arrived in New York that summer. Sally was the best pal a boy could have—she ran, climbed, and drove a mean Big Wheel. She played so rough that I doubted Matthew thought of Sally as a girl.

But one December day before Sally's birthday, I found out otherwise.

As we drove by the turnoff to Sally's house, Matthew stared down the street. "I want to get Sally a birthday present," he declared.

No problem, I thought. Footballs were easy to find.

"What do you want to get her?"

"A dress."

I nearly wrecked the van. *"Really?* A dress?"

"Yes. I want to get her a pretty dress. She needs a pretty dress."

In the following days, I tried to dissuade him. I wasn't ready to be Casanova's mother. But his desire grew; by the time we got to the thrift store, he was hunting for a "pretty silver dress that shined in the sunlight."

There were no silver dresses, but he was undaunted. Like a Fifth Avenue merchandiser, he compared styles and stitching. Heart-shaped buttons, nice. Had a spot, no good.

I watched in amazement. I was rearing a sensitive nineties guy. I wasn't ready.

He settled on a red print dress with white trim, three-quarter-length sleeves, and dropped waistline.

We washed and wrapped the treasured dress. He made a card: "Dear Sally, I hope you have a happy birthday. I hope you like my present."

Sally wore the dress to church the next day. It fit perfectly. And while it didn't shine, Sally did.

And Matthew did, too.

That was six years ago. The dress is in my attic. Sally lives in Illinois and has outgrown tomboyhood.

And Matthew has met another athletic girl with the same birthday.

Last week he was at it again, shopping for something silver or shiny. He found jewelry.

Someday, it's going to be diamonds.

And I'm not going to be ready.

. . .

The day is coming so quickly, Lord,
when I'll lose the boy You've given me to another woman.
Please make me ready for that time,
and help me make him ready.

I will therefore that the younger women marry,
bear children, guide the house,
give none occasion to the adversary
to speak reproachfully.
1 TIMOTHY 5:14

I am an awful mother.

Now understand, I would not ordinarily do such a thing. I respect my children's privacy and property. I usually let their stuff alone.

But I had to paint their bedroom (aka "The Kline Street Dump"). And I had to move their stuff. Lots and lots of stuff.

Clothes. Toys. Golf tees. Magazines. Tags from the clothes Grandma sent. Discarded paragraphs from a report. An outline for said report. The other sock. Wires. Earphones. Building blocks.

In addition to their already-filled junk boxes, I filled at least a half-dozen sacks with odds and ends.

And as I did—oh, I am an awful mother—I was overcome with an urge to throw out stuff. And, well, they weren't home, so I did!

Out went the scribbled papers, the clothes tags, the outline, the obvious junk. But I was careful not to trash anything they might have been saving for some reason.

After all, I was a kid once. I was a pack rat. I saved anything that I might use "someday" and everything that reminded me of someone or something.

I saved all the notes I got from Angela in eighth grade. I had a chain made out of chewing gum wrappers and a stash of wrappers to add to it. I had an ice-cream carton full of smiley buttons.

But there is a difference between their kid stuff and my kid stuff. My kid stuff was organized.

Angela's notes were in ice-cream cartons on the third shelf of the northeast cupboard; the wrapper chain was over the doorway; the wrapper stash and smiley buttons were in the southeast cupboard.

Unlike me, my junkmeisters have no method in their madness. They just have stuff—and it all stays wherever it falls.

And that drives me nuts. If they're going to have junk, fine. But at least they ought to know what they have and where it goes.

Even so, I do respect their right to their stuff, however messy. And I promise never to throw out any item that has recognized value to them.

Well, maybe.

After sweeping their floor a hundred times, I was crawling on my knees when I came upon a little bitty Lego piece.

I looked at it once, then twice. And then—oh, please, forgive me—*I threw it away!*

I am an awful mother.

And I love it.

Often it's difficult to
rule this household You've given me, Lord.
Give me the courage to do what is right,
to train and discipline my children,
and to teach them to keep themselves
and their possessions in order.

So likewise ye, when ye shall have done
all those things which
are commanded you,
say, We are unprofitable servants:
we have done that which was our duty to do.
LUKE 17:10

I'm on strike!

I've picked up my last pair of dirty undies, my last fermented sock. Kid mess is not my problem anymore. It's theirs. And they're going to solve it.

1. I am no longer going to fold their clothes.
    I'll wash and sort, but if they want folded
    clothes in drawers, they'll have to do it
    themselves.

    One morning I reminded the younger ones of this.
    "What?!" one protested. "I just folded and put away clothes a few days ago! I don't want to have to do that *forever!!*"
    Neither do I. And since I'm bigger, I'm not going to anymore.

2. I am not going to take out the kitchen trash.
    And I'm not going to beg and plead to have
    it done. I'm also not going to make any
    clever signs to put on the can (*"real men* take

out the trash without being told").

If they don't do it, I won't do anything in the kitchen to generate more trash. (I'll stop cooking.)

3. I will not pick up their rooms. It's their space. It's their problem. If they want to be slobs, they can live with their mess. In fact, they can stay in their mess, confined to quarters until they shape up.
4. I will no longer repeat myself. Do you hear me? I am no longer going to repeat myself! And that's final. Understand?
5. As concerns other various duties that can be handled by someone younger than twenty: I quit.

Am I shirking my motherly duties? Not at all. Part of my job is to train them to be dependable and independent. In too many areas, they've been pampered. It's time they all started contributing.

Besides, this is for their own good. Someday (sooner than I desire) they'll be on their own. And then one day, Lord willing, they'll be married.

How many marriages have started disintegrating because a husband couldn't find the hamper or a wife couldn't boil water?

God forbid a future daughter- or son-in-law says to one of mine: "Didn't your mother ever teach you how to pick up your underwear?" Why, I'd die of embarrassment.

If I do for them what they really can do for themselves, I do them a disservice.

Changing their habits won't be easy.

But the price is too high if they don't.

I can't afford to strike out.

. . .

As Your servant,
I desire to do my duty in all areas of life.
It is my duty to rule my house,
to manage my children wisely,
to teach them what their duty is.
Give me the right amount of stubbornness
to be faithful to this duty.
And give me grace,
so we all can bear the cost of this obedience.

*Before I formed thee
in the belly I knew thee.*
JEREMIAH 1:5

1998

In 1983, my friend Carolyn had a precious little boy. Billy was tiny and sick at birth. For sixteen days, Billy fought for life with his parents at his side.

"The only place I wanted to be was with my child," Carolyn said. "I never realized what an instinct God has given mothers to hold their babies close to them, and how intense it is. At times I felt almost sick over not being able to hold him."

Carolyn held Billy once, on the last day. With life supports removed, she gathered him in her arms and felt his little life drain away.

I was married but childless then. While I shared Carolyn's sorrow, I really didn't understand why her arms ached so much to hold her baby when she already had two children.

Five years after that, I understood. I had a miscarriage. My arms felt so empty.

Soon thereafter, another life began in me. This little one made me sick for twelve weeks. It was a good sickness, because I knew he was growing.

When I started feeling better, we discovered the baby had died. Eventually, I had to let him be taken from my body.

And I had no baby to hold, no baby to bury. I grieved as my arms ached.

Before that pain had subsided, there was one more miscarriage. I thought I'd never hold another newborn.

But I eventually did. I held five more. My arms were full and happy.

Then two weeks ago, after two months of tightening waistbands and upset stomachs, I was told the preposterous: I was pregnant, but there was no baby. Several days later, I found myself in the emergency room as the pregnancy resolved itself.

Though surrounded by children, my arms hurt again. I knew why.

It's as a mother of nine said as she was miscarrying, "As soon as you find out you're pregnant, it's a baby."

To a mother's heart, it's a baby, a little person with great potential. It's someone to love. Someone to hold.

And when you lose a baby, you can't help but wonder—and ache.

While lying on the couch recovering, my angel snuggled close and gave me a kiss. "Hug me," she said.

"Why?"

"Because I'm your daughter, and you wuv me."

I squeezed her.

"I wuv you," she said.

With that kind of love, I know the ache will fade away.

Father, You have put within my mother's heart
a love for all my children—
even those yet to be born. I know them before they are born.
And when You take them before their births,
I cannot help but grieve.
Yet I must trust Your perfect will in these losses.
You will not give me less than Your best.
This, too, will make me more like Christ.
Comfort my heart in this, so I may comfort others.

It is vain for you to rise up early, to sit up late, to eat
the bread of sorrows:
for so he giveth his beloved sleep.
PSALM 127:2

A friend and I
were discussing our busy lives.

She said she had a plan to keep outside commitments
to a minimum.

"Put a sign by the phone," she said: " 'Just say no!' "

It was good advice, which I intended to take.

But I never made the sign.

I was too busy.

The time has come. I am going to slow down.

Even as I write that, I am filled with trepidation.
I have been going so fast for so long that just thinking
about stopping makes my palms sweat.

I wasn't always this way. As a child, I was often
lazy. But I watched my busy mother "do it all." And
by high school, I, too, did everything I could do. I
thought "could" meant "should." Because I never said
"no," I was given many things to do. I became a very
busy teenager.

I grew into a busy adult. After college and before
kids, I worked two or three jobs—just for something
to do.

Having children didn't change me, it just changed
what I did. Instead of jobs, there were endless chores

219

and errands. The third baby spent so much time on the road, she thought the nursery had bucket seats and four-on-the-floor.

In 1997, I slowed down accidentally. I broke my leg (delivering newspapers with my son) and spent six weeks on the couch. It changed my perspective.

I saw that doing the mother stuff isn't as important as being the mother. That time should be invested, not just spent. That "could" and "should" are not equivalent. That when mothers are driven, kids sometimes get run over.

Yet once I was well, I went back to my old ways, desperately trying to "catch up" on the time and activities lost.

One of these days, I will slow down. I will say "no." I will read more, laugh more, pray more.

And I will start now.

Just as soon as I dry my palms.

. . .

Help me, Father. My desire is to slow down,
to invest and redeem the time You have given me,
to enjoy all there is to life on this earth.
Yet my nature is not slow.
It is driven, hyper, anxious, and sometime neurotic.
Remind me of the folly of such a life.
Slow me down, Lord.
Let me enjoy the sleep You give.

Return unto thy rest, O my soul;
for the LORD hath dealt bountifully with thee.
PSALM 116:7

"You," Mom said, *"are your own worst enemy."*
I heard this observation many times in my childhood. And I know it was true.

For example, growing up I rarely had a playmate. I'd complain and Mom would say, "Call somebody and go play." But I wouldn't call. And then I'd pout.

Or I'd come home from school upset because someone had teased me. I rarely had a snappy comeback, so instead of dismissing an ugly comment, I'd let it stew in my brain, hurting me all over again.

Yes, Mom was right: I really was my own worst enemy.

And I still am.

Although I have outgrown many childhood weaknesses, I still add to my own frustrations. In fact, I create most of my problems.

Take our puppy (please!). We kept one of the puppies of Stubbie, our boonie dog. This puppy was the one I had had to hand feed because his mother had injured him. Having so mothered the puppy, I didn't want to give him away.

But now he's getting too big for a household with eight children. So now I'm faced with the heartache of finding him a new home.

Yet if I had taken his mother to the shelter before

she went into heat, I wouldn't have had any puppies to fret over.

Right now, I'm very frustrated over the clutter in my house. It's so bad, I don't know where to begin. Yet so much of it is my fault. I get myself so busy that I feel too rushed to file papers or put things away. I think I'll get back to them "later," but when "later" comes, there's some other activity or crisis to attend to.

If I'd just say "no" to some things (even some good things), I wouldn't be as rushed and I could deal with the junk mail, correspondence, and lazy kids in a more timely and orderly way.

I know there is a solution. The cure for a worst enemy is a Best Friend. God is a God of simplicity, order, and rest. I know that as I focus on Him, He will give me the strength to clean up the house. And He will give me the rest I need.

Speaking of rest, I'd better get to bed.

Those cute little chicks I bought the kids turned into noisy roosters that get up before the sun. . . .

. . .

Oh, Lord, let me understand this truth:
You are a bountiful God. All the gifts You give—
even the mere breath of life—
show Your bounty to me.
It is silly to strive as I do,
when I can and should rest in You.

And when she came to her mother in law, she said,
Who art thou, my daughter?
RUTH 3:16

There are days!

Days when the sibling rivalries escalate into sibling wars.

Days when light bulbs blow and washers walk, when little hearts break at every whispered "no."

Days when things go so bad my friends wonder if I've broken a chain letter.

Such days remind me of my first boss, a single mother. Every day, she handled the stress of the newsroom; every night, the challenge of rearing two boys alone. One evening while I was helping her with household duties, she sighed: "Every mother needs a mother."

Now I know how right she was. We mothers who comfort the hurting, lift up the downcast, hear the heartbeats, direct the aimless, and teach the ignorant sometimes—often—need someone to comfort, uplift, hear, direct, and teach us. In short, we mothers need mothers.

God knew this; He programmed us this way. Older women are to "teach the young women to be sober, to love their husbands, to love their children, to be discreet, chaste, keepers at home. . . ."

Mothers are the ideal older women. But some of us no longer have mothers or have moved far away from them. If we want mothers, we have to borrow them. My mother-in-law is my perennial long-distance mother, who is always just a phone call or an E-mail away.

But one summer, a friend loaned me her mother in an "up close and personal" way. This dear woman, who is gifted at decorating, knows I am not. For months, she sent wallpaper samples for me to consider, until she found the perfect print. Then when she was visiting her daughter, she spent a day and a half hanging it for me.

On the second day, she also did grandma duty while I went to a morning-long appointment. I got home frustrated, overwhelmed, and in tears.

She hugged me, listened, empathized, and encouraged, just like my own mom. That didn't solve any problems for me, but I was comforted, and I knew things would work out.

Yes, every mother does need a mother.

Even if it's not her own.

. . .

You've given me so many mothers since
You took my own mother home.
I am grateful for the time, love,
and encouragement they've given me.
Now that I am older,
let me encourage younger women to live godly lives.
Let me be the older woman I should be.

But why dost thou judge thy brother?
or why dost thou set at nought thy brother?
for we shall all stand before
the judgment seat of Christ.
ROMANS 14:10

One fall in Aberdeen,

there were two conferences that caught my attention.

Early in October, a group that advocated home birth met quietly at the Holiday Inn. Hardly anyone noticed. In fact, the conference center fouled up the reservation and the first evening the group (of non-smoking, nondrinking, Bible-believers) gathered in a downstairs lounge area that reeked of cigarette smoke.

Later that month, businesswomen met at a more glitzy conference, dubbed "Reach for the Stars," which overtook the Ramkota. The media paid attention to this one, and it was well attended.

On the surface, the meetings had little in common.

At the first, the women (mostly at-home mothers) and several men heard a speaker—a man—promote a no-contraceptive lifestyle called the "Full Quiver." Babies nursed as their mothers listened. One participant began labor. She went home and had her baby before the conference ended.

At the second meeting, the women discussed success in the workplace. They applauded women who have excelled in business and politics. They "networked."

They went home challenged and excited.

Because I was an at-home mother who freelanced for the newspaper, I was at both conferences.

To my surprise, they had several things in common.

Of the at-home mothers, several ran or assisted in home-based businesses. Of the businesswomen, most were mothers.

The women at the first meeting wanted freedom—freedom to have their babies at home with a midwife; freedom to do the best possible job rearing children.

Those at the second also wanted freedom—freedom to work and achieve without gender constraints; freedom to do the best job possible.

Given the similarities, I wondered why the meetings had almost no attendees in common. I met only one other woman at Reach for the Stars who had been at the birth conference.

I believe it has to do with the perceptions we women have of each other: We either stay at home or we go to work (and never the twain shall meet). Sometimes, we even view each other with suspicion.

That's unfortunate. Because as women we're not all that different. Where we choose to spend our energies varies, but our fears and struggles and aspirations are very similar.

We're all reaching for the stars.

They're just in different galaxies.

It is a shame that even in Christian circles,
we women are split on this issue, Father.
Let us not judge one another,
but let us encourage one another to serve You
as we are fully persuaded in our own minds.

For the children ought not to lay up for the parents,
but the parents for the children.
And I will very gladly spend and be spent for you.
2 CORINTHIANS 12:14–15

I remember when I first beheld my firstborn, Matthew.

He was born by C-section, so I couldn't touch him. Instead, Mike got to hold him and carry him to the nursery. I watched from the operating table and smiled at my baby.

My baby. Oh, the miracle of creating a new life! Oh the excitement of having a new person to mold and lead and love! Why, it was more than my groggy brain could comprehend.

Soon enough the anesthesia wore off and reality set in.

Here was a new life. A new life that needed to be fed and clothed and changed, again and again and again.

Here was a new person, who had his own likes and dislikes, who had a mind of his own, and was not afraid to express himself loudly.

And here was a new challenge. Often I was confounded by the tiny life I had begotten. Why did he cry like that? What was the matter this time? What was I doing wrong?

More than once I wished he had come with instructions tattooed to his bottom. It would have made things so much easier: "Wash daily, in lukewarm water; pat dry; hug frequently; feed every two to four hours, depending on appetite; wrap snugly; sing to freely. When all else fails, invest in ear plugs."

But alas, he didn't come with directions, or with a warning label, which I could have really used: "Warning: Your accountant has determined that this little life will cost you a pretty penny and maybe your sanity. Start saving both today."

While we've kept kid expenses down over the years —we don't buy designer clothes or expensive toys— there have been many unforeseen, though not totally unexpected, costs over the years. Trips to emergency rooms for gashed faces and hands; trips to the doctor and dentist.

And now we're adding another—trips to the ortho-dontist. Ouch!

Like all the other challenges and expenses of child-rearing, we'll manage this one. It may strain things for awhile, but we'll survive, as millions of other parents of mangled-mouth teens have. I hope.

I wish I had foreseen how much parenthood would cost. It would have been good to go into it with eyes wide open.

On second thought, maybe it's better that we look upon our babies in love and not knowledge.

If we'd known, we might not have loved enough to make the sacrifice.

Father, I'm glad it was—and still is—
impossible to count the cost of rearing children.
If I had had any real idea of how much it would be,
I might have looked at myself
and rejected the blessings You had for me.
But as it is, I can only look to You to provide.
Thank You for enabling us to care for our children.

And the Lord said unto Moses,
I will do this thing also that thou hast spoken:
for thou hast found grace in my sight,
and I know thee by name.
EXODUS 33:17

In 1984, I got a new name.

In one brief moment, I went from being "Helen" to being "Mommy." It seemed fitting. My whole existence had been changed by the arrival of a little boy. Why not my name?

At first, this seemed a good thing. I was a mother, Matthew's mother. But "Mother" was too stuffy. "Mommy" was just right. I liked it, and I liked knowing who I was.

Now I'm not so sure. While I think I'm "Mommy," the kids seem to think I'm someone else.

In the beginning, I was not "Mommy" but *"Waahhh."* Whenever Matthew cried, *"Waahhh,"* I responded.

Sooner than expected, I became "Mama." Sometimes "Ma." And sometimes, "Mamamamamamama."

This was fine, too. And usually cute.

By the time Matthew hit two, I was really "Mommy." I was Mommy who played games, Mommy who went for walks. Mommy who could fix everything. Mommy who took him to the ice cream parlor to watch the choo-choo train. Mommy. Mommy. Mommy.

At last we both knew who I was. He identified me over and over and over again.

I was still "Mommy" to Matthew when I became *"waahhh"* and "Mama" to John. That was sometimes difficult to keep straight, but we managed until I was "Mommy" to both. (But by then, I was *"waahhh"* to Jane.)

"Mommy" was my name for a long time, but slowly it was changing. Matthew and I both grew older. And then I was just "Mom." (Though I was still "Mommy" to Jane and *"waahhh"* to Charles.)

I liked "Mom." It was the perfect mother name. Pithy. Palindromic. Easy on the ears. Went well with apple pie.

Matthew and I worked well with "Mom." And gradually the younger ones realized it was a good name. We were all happy with it.

But then Matthew turned thirteen. His gray matter got scattered, and his mouth got loose. And my name changed again.

"You need to make your bed," I'd say. And he'd say, "Ahhh, Maahhhmm."

One day he stared at my head. *"Maahhhmm!* You have gray hair!!"

Often I catch a hint of teenaged condescension in "Maahhhmm." Apparently "Maahhhmm" is not as smart as "Mommy" and "Mom" were. I don't like being "Maahhhmm."

One day, I told little Ben to clean his plate. He looked at me and said, "Maahhhmmm!"

"That's 'Mommy' to YOU," I snapped.

At least one of them needs to know who I am.

. . .

Father, sometimes my children do not know who I am.
And sometimes I don't know who I am either.
But I am grateful that
because I have found grace in Your sight,
You know me by name.

Strength and honour are her clothing;
and she shall rejoice in time to come.

PROVERBS 31:25

One lovely Guam day,
we went to the beach with
another homeschooling family.
While the mama of the family attended to their new-born, the dad did daddy duty watching his little ones—ages two to five—in the water.

He spent the time on his knees in the shallows, holding his preschoolers by the hands or skimming them across the water on their bellies. With Daddy holding her, his five year old was a big girl swimming in the big, blue ocean.

Afterward, he threw his towel over his shoulders and sighed. "The way I figure it," he said thoughtfully, "I'll be fifty before I can swim by myself again."

Fifty!

Lucky man.

I'll be sixty before I can do almost anything by myself again.

And in the meantime, I will dream about that day.

— That day when I can go to the bathroom alone, without a little person peeking in the door to tell me he's found his marble.
— That day when I can sit down for an

entire meal, eat it before it reaches room temperature, and digest it without having to first clean up a two-year-old face.
— That day when I can cut my food only.
— That day when the floor stays swept, the refrigerator door stays shut, the towels stay on the rack.
— That day when everything will be organized, when my pen stays where I put it and doesn't walk around the house.
— That day when I can—"Put the T-shirt in the hamper, Anna"—finish a sentence without talking to a kid.
— That day when I can eat all of my dessert; when I can use crystal and wear silk.

Sigh.
It sounds delightful.
Peaceful.
Predictable.
Lonely.

Although a house without children—an empty nest —seems attractive now, I know that when it comes, I'll be longing for the good old days.

And I'll be waiting eagerly for the first sign of the minivan coming up the road, filled with my grandbabies.

And I'll probably laugh when the grandest grand-baby in the world burps up his lunch—and it goes down my back.

And I'll enjoy every fussy, messy moment and cry when they leave.

So why can't I enjoy it now?

Well, I do.

Most of the time, I'm happy with my little ones around me. I feel privileged and blessed.

Sometimes, though, I'd like to set the table with crystal.

But I'll probably never wear silk.

. . .

*Let me not wait for today's trials
to become tomorrow's blessings.
Rather let me enjoy what You've given me today.
The future is Yours. Only this moment is mine.*

Casting down imaginations,
and every high thing that exalteth itself
against the knowledge of God,
and bringing into captivity every thought
to the obedience of Christ.
2 CORINTHIANS 10:5

Back in the idyllic B.C.
(before children) days of marriage,

I had a rosy picture of motherhood.

A mother, I thought, was one who cherished her children, who nurtured them physically, mentally, and spiritually. A mother laughed and played with her children. She was there to tickle and kiss and hug.

Mother was a pied piper, able to play a mystical tune that would make her little ones fall in line and follow wherever she led.

Mother had perfect timing. In seconds, she could wipe away the hurt of nasty words. She knew when to dish up gentle criticisms and when to dish up home-made apple pie.

She was a magician. She could heal a bruised knee with a kiss or make cooked carrots irresistible. She made Jell-O seem like dessert at a five-star restaurant.

Mother was the unsung, behind-the-scenes hero-ine of innumerable battles. It was her love, her cour-age, her confidence in her children that inspired those children and led them to victory, whether the challenge was on the playground or on a battlefield.

With all my heart I believed that "the hand that rocks the cradle rules the nation."

But then I had children.

While I've cherished my children, sometimes I've been too tired to nurture them. I've laughed at them and with them, but I've also cried over them.

I've tried to play a tune, but instead of following, they sit on the couch and say, "What can I do, Mom? There's nothing to do."

My timing is lousy. When they nearly break their necks bouncing on the bed, instead of comforting them, I say, "Well, you know you're not supposed to jump on beds." When they are screaming bloody murder outside my bathroom door, I scream back: "ARE YOU BLEEDING?"

When I put carrots on the table, they say, "YUCK! Carrots again?!"

In my house, the hand that rocks the cradle gets splinters.

The ideal mother I'm not.

But the truth is, there are no perfect mothers. Never have been. Never will be.

We are all humans, all flawed. All gaining wisdom through on-the-job training. All prone to make mistakes.

Fortunately, success in motherhood lies not in perfection, but in humility. It's the mother who sees her mistakes and corrects them (and corrects her children) that will eventually succeed.

And in the meantime, it certainly doesn't hurt to laugh.

· · ·

Father, I have been guilty of lifting up my
imaginations of motherhood higher
than they ought to have been lifted.
I've even worshiped that ideal by looking to it for guidance.
I know I should only look to You for direction.
Please give me strength to keep my eyes on You.

Like as a woman with child,
that draweth near the time of her delivery,
is in pain, and crieth out in her pangs. . .
ISAIAH 26:17

A new Middlebrooke should arrive in about five weeks.

Some women—those who have never had a baby—have said, "It's just around the corner."

Others—those with children—sigh knowingly. They know that the last month of pregnancy is the longest. A virtual eternity. The month of the longest days.

And even longer nights.

In the last two months, most of my nights have been spent on the couch. Or somewhere between the couch and the bathroom.

A typical night is spent in sleep limbo—I lie half awake, half asleep, thinking of all the things I don't have time to think about during the day: Where will I put this new kid? Should I get anything out of storage yet? Should I confidently get out the girl stuff, or just wait to see?

I roll over. My back hurts.

I fling back the sheet—I'm too hot.

I roll back.

I fumble for the blanket—I'm chilled.

The bladder alarm rings. Only 12:30. I can already

tell it's going to be a long night.

I stumble toward the bathroom, then stumble back to the couch.

OUCH!

I trip over the fan.

It's going to be a very long night.

I plop down again.

I rearrange the pillows and covers. I elevate the legs while trying to support the back. How can one body get so disunited in nine months? If I soothe one area, another area hurts.

I finally get comfortable. But then my wombmate wakes and starts rearranging furniture. *Ba-doomp. Ba-doomp. Tapita-tapita-tapita-tapita.*

Outside, the neighborhood dogs call their nightly convention to order. I listen for our dog—as long as she's quiet, I can ignore the ruckus.

I close my eyes.

Ba-doomp. Tapita-tapita-tapita.

"Go to sleep, Baby," I say.

Ba-doomp.

The bladder alarm goes off again. Only 2 A.M.!

This is going to be a very, very, long night.

Eventually, between the alarms, I rest.

Suddenly, I stretch. My leg cramps. OUCH!

I stretch it slowly and wince. Only five more weeks.

I roll over. I sense a brightness.

Is that the light at the end of the tunnel?

No. It's just the sun, rising much too early for this tired mama.

Sigh.

Only five more weeks. . .

. . .

*Lord, I thought I had said,
"Give me patience," not, "give me pregnancy."
Yet You know what is best for me.
Please give me the grace I need to
allow patience to be developed in me.*

And Mary said,
Behold the handmaid of the Lord;
be it unto me according to thy word.
LUKE 1:38

"Mary said. . ."
Mary, the one who found favor with God.
The "blessed virgin."
The mother of the Son of God.
The mother, revered through the ages.
This Mary speaks.
"Behold. . ."
Look here. See. Observe. Pay attention.
"The handmaid. . ."
The female slave.
A servant.
One with no rights of her own.
One who takes orders.
". . .of the Lord."
But not just anyone's slave.
God's slave.
God, though demanding, is ever merciful.
"Be it unto me according to thy word."
Give me what You will, as You have said.
I am willing to accept the task You have promised.
I will obey.

For Mary, obedience meant a loss of reputation. The one

favored by God would know man's rejection and scorn.

As a sword would pierce His side, a sword would pierce her heart.

Having the world's only perfect child would not make her the perfect mother. She would need His salvation.

Like Mary, I need the Son's salvation. And I take it willingly.

But can I be like Mary? Am I a willing slave? Can I withstand the scorn of the world because God says I should be a "keeper at home," under the authority of my own husband?

Am I willing to make the sacrifice called motherhood?

Will I obey? How can I?

As Mary did.

By faith.

In the Word of God.

Father, my heart's desire is
to submit to Your calling to motherhood,
but it is so difficult in a world that
sees my choice as contemptible.
Remind me that it was no easier for Mary—
as the mother of Your Son,
she was despised by the world from the start.
As You blessed her for her obedience,
so You will bless me for mine.

BEING
CHANGED BY GOD'S
SPECIAL BLESSING. . .

Sometimes, God's hand is very obvious in our lives. On February 19, 2000, He gave us a special blessing, a little girl, who is changing us all and is teaching us of His wonderful love and grace.

As arrows are in the hand of a mighty man;
so are children of the youth.
Happy is the man that hath his quiver full of them.
PSALM 127:4–5

Summer 1998

Pity poor Benjamin.

Here he is, not yet two, barely talking, and already his siblings are starting a movement to have him dethroned as the Reigning Baby.

His favorite big sister, Jane, started the insurrection one afternoon. She came into the office, plopped on a chair, and watched me work. Then, when the moment was just right, she innocently lobbed the verbal grenade.

"Mom?" she said quietly. "When are you going to have another baby?"

Ka-boom!

"What?!"

"You're fat enough to be having a baby."

"Well, the nerve of some people's children! You try having seven babies and see what happens to your tummy. You're not always going to be skinny!"

"Sorry, Mom," she said. Having accomplished her mission, she left quickly.

A day or two later, the barrage began. This time, it was started by the Sassy One. This time, I counter-attacked.

"Mommy," Anna said, "are you going to have another baby?"

"Maybe one of these days," I said nonchalantly.

"What's the baby's name going to be?"

"Deborah Helen."

"Guys!" she screamed as she ran down the hall, *"Mom's gonna have a baby named Debwah Hellinn!"*

"Deborah Helen?" Charles said. "A girl! When?" He was indignant. He promptly came to my room to discuss the matter.

"Why a girl?" he demanded. "I want a boy! Dad likes boys!"

"Dad likes girls, too. Besides, we have enough boys. And I need a baby named after me."

He thought a minute then turned to leave. "I want a boy," he said firmly.

Anna came back.

"When you get a new baby, are you gonna get rid of Ben?"

"I kept you when I got Ben, didn't I?"

Miraculously, the discussion ended there. But it was not forgotten. The next morning, Anna started again: "What's the name of the baby going to be?"

I told her, and she went away happily.

But I was rattled. In this family, talking about babies is dangerous. All it seems to take is a word and— surprise!

In 1991, for example, one of them prayed for a

new baby during Children's Church. Two weeks later I was pregnant. If the whole bunch starts wishing and praying for another sibling, I'm in trouble. I'd better not sell the maternity clothes yet.

Seriously, I know the kids are just being silly.

But until the baby talk subsides, Mike is sleeping on the couch.

. . .

*I am so blessed to be the mother of so many.
And if You choose to send me another child,
let me not be afraid.
You will provide the means
to care for the child You send.*

Many, O Lord my God,
are thy wonderful works which thou hast done,
and thy thoughts which are to us-ward:
they cannot be reckoned up in order unto thee:
if I would declare and speak of them,
they are more than can be numbered.

PSALM 40:5

I couldn't have been much more than three years old when Uncle Charlie began my training in his favorite sport—baseball.

For many happy hours in my childhood I stood by the plate, swinging at pitch after pitch after pitch. By the time I was able to hold my 28-inch wooden bat, I could clobber and field a softball deftly. I was pretty good for a girl. Uncle Charlie's smile told me so.

But hitting and fielding were not all I learned in Uncle Charlie's outdoor classroom.

When I struck out, I had to be brave enough not to whine. Then I had to have the perseverance to pick up the bat to try again.

When the ball was just out of my grasp, I had to have the courage to reach for it.

And sometimes I just had to go with what came and do my best.

I'm glad I learned the lessons of baseball. Now I know that if I strike out at something, life isn't over; I'll have another chance at bat.

Early in 2000, life threw me a curve ball.

On February 19 at 8 P.M., Deborah Helen Middlebrooke arrived thirteen days ahead of schedule. She was tiny for a Middlebrooke—7 lb. 3 oz. She came with red hair.

And she came with an extra chromosome.

Deborah has Down syndrome.

Within eight hours of birth, she had some problems that suggested she had a heart defect. Before she was thirty-six hours old, she took her first plane ride to the U.S. Naval Hospital in Okinawa, Japan.

While in the Land of the Rising Sun, it rained every day.

But in the Neonatal Intensive Care Unit, the Son shone on Deborah. Her heart and all the other organs that can be affected by Down syndrome were found to be normal. It took awhile for her lungs to work exactly right, but they straightened out in time.

But what of the Down syndrome itself?

I'll have to handle that the way Uncle Charlie taught me to handle any curve ball. Watch it carefully. Then step into it and swing. No whining. Just courage. Perseverance. Patience.

Life is not over. We must go on.

Deborah's game has just begun.

Father, I do not know what Your thoughts were
when You sent Deborah to us,
but I know they were good thoughts.
I know Deborah is no mistake.
You called her into being;
You gave her to us to fulfill Your purposes.
You are working out something marvelous here.
Give me eyes to see it.

Call unto me, and I will answer thee,
and shew thee great and mighty things,
which thou knowest not.
JEREMIAH 33:3

I leaned over the warming bed, staring at my poor little one.

At first glance, there appeared to be more equipment than baby. She lay beneath an oxygen hood; from head to foot, she was tubed and wired.

I picked up the little hand that was free and massaged it gently.

A nurse joined me. She stared a moment, then asked The Question.

"Did you know before she was born?"

"I refused all those tests that would have shown it," I said. "But I knew in my heart. God told me."

She was a Christian and she understood. But many people don't understand and don't believe me when I tell them that. But it is true.

God started telling me about Deborah the night He gave me her name. I was sitting in my bedroom in South Dakota, thinking about my children, and I sensed God saying, "I'm going to give you another girl. She's going to be special."

Like many people, I long to hear God speak. But when He said something I wasn't eager to hear, I thought maybe it wasn't God after all.

But as the months passed, I knew it had been God, because He kept speaking.

A friend gave me a novel about a mother who had a daughter (Brenda Kay) with Down syndrome in the 1940s. While reading the book on the plane to Guam, a phrase caught my attention, and I stopped. "Lord," I whispered. "Why am I reading this?" And that same, patient Spirit seemed to answer, "Just pay attention."

Several months later, my eye fell on a newspaper article that was the transcript of a speech given by a seventh-grader with Down syndrome. It was a better speech than most "normal" students could give.

"See—they can learn, they can excel," the Spirit said.

By this time, I was pregnant. As the pregnancy progressed, little things told me something was different. Then the baby stopped moving, and all I could think of was a line from the book, "Brenda Kay slept."

Then, during an ultrasound, I saw her eye, and I knew.

By the time Deborah arrived, I knew God had sent her as He had said.

And I was blessed.

For I knew the One who had sent was the One who had spoken.

And I knew He would sustain.

It is my desire to keep
my heart and ears open to You, Father.
Thank You for persisting when
my ears were dull and
for giving me a new little reason
to listen in the future.

And he said unto me,
My grace is sufficient for thee:
for my strength is made perfect in weakness.
Most gladly therefore will I rather
glory in my infirmities,
that the power of Christ may rest upon me.

2 CORINTHIANS 12:9

A week into our stay in Okinawa, everything seemed to be going wrong.

Although Deborah's heart was fine, it appeared her lungs were abnormal. She could not maintain the oxygen level in her blood. Try as they did, the doctors couldn't find any cause for it.

Her thyroid hormone levels were unusual, so she kept getting stuck for blood tests. And her electrolytes were questionable, so she needed intravenous supplementation, which meant having an IV site somewhere on her body. It seemed nurses were always hovering over her, trying to put in a new site because the old one had failed. (She had so many IVs taped to her head, I was sure she was going to go home bald.)

Every time they stuck her, she yelled, and I wanted to. Inside, the mother-part of me was screaming, *"Get your hands off my baby!"* while my mouth cooed, "I'm sorry, Sweetheart. This will help you get better."

The frustration was overwhelming. I so wanted her to get better; I so wanted to take her home. I wanted to touch her and make her whole; I wanted to fix her. But I couldn't.

To make matters worse, the U.S. Consulate had misplaced part of my passport application. I could not leave Japan without a passport. And I couldn't get it myself; I had to trust a young man at the hospital to help.

That day, as I walked through the rain back to the parents' cottage, it was wetter beneath the umbrella.

"I can't do anything!" I cried through hot tears. *"I can't fix anything. I'm alone. . . I'm broken. . . Is this where you want me, Father?!"*

Even in my frustration, I knew I was exactly where He wanted me.

I was at the end of myself.

It is at the end of "self" that God does His greatest work, because it is there that we are willing to let Him.

And so I got out of the way and watched Him work.

Though I had more moments of weakness and unbelief after that, God remained faithful. He demonstrated His power and love for us by working out all those things that were beyond my power.

He showed me that He would take care of His special child.

That He was in control.

That even when life goes wrong, He can make it right.

Father, the "wrong" times show me
how right life is for Your child.
Thank You for taking me to the end of myself
and sustaining me there.
You have shown me Your power;
You have shown me Yourself.
I pray I will never lose sight of You again.

Rest in the LORD,
and wait patiently for him.
PSALM 37:7

Deborah and I returned home to Guam from Okinawa on her due date, March 3, 2000.

Our twelve-day stay in Japan was anything but a vacation. There was no time to take in the wonder and beauty of an unknown place; I barely had time to shop for souvenirs. My days were spent in the hospital with Deborah. My brief nights were spent in the parents' house on the grounds.

The schedule was hard enough, but life was even harder because it was the first time I had been away from my family for an extended time. My heart was torn in two.

I felt like Dorothy in Oz. From the moment we found out Deborah's heart looked fine (about an hour after arriving), my goal was to get us home.

But it was a goal I could not reach. All I could do was wait on the Lord to work things out in His time.

And did He ever work! Even before we left Guam, prayers were answered. I was allowed to fly into Japan with an expired passport.

Once there, His hand never left us.

He gave me favor in the eyes of a hospital clerk, who processed my passport application even though I had been told she processed baby passports only.

He sent people to help. A friend of a friend fed me twice and took me to church. She also found me a free car seat for the trip home.

He gave me support in the Neonatal Unit itself. Another couple from Guam, whose little boy had been born very early, became my friends. One of the NICU technicians was from Bristol, South Dakota, and had grown up in a church in Aberdeen, our last home.

The Lord gave grace to Deborah throughout. He made all of her systems "kick in" at just the right time. He blessed her sluggish lungs with a remarkable recovery, which led one doctor to say Deborah was a "miracle baby."

Of all the miracles surrounding us, the most obvious one came the last morning.

Because of a mix-up at the U.S. Consulate, my passport had been delayed. It was to be delivered around 9 A.M. Friday morning, the day I planned to leave.

Ordinarily this would not have been a problem, because the Guam flight usually takes off around 10 A.M. But this Friday, the plane was to leave early at 8:15!

I found this out at 6:30 A.M., when there was no one in the hospital who could help. I looked pleadingly at the Aerovac clerk: "Look, I need to get home today and I don't have ruby slippers to get me there. Isn't there anyone who can help me?" He shrugged.

Again, God was our only hope. Tearfully, I called Mike to have him pray.

The moment after I put down the phone, the one person who could help was in the hall. He said, "We'll delay the plane until you get your passport."

And he did! I got my passport at 8:45, and we were homeward bound by 9:30.

We got to Guam in the early afternoon. It was sunny and hot. We took the kids for pizza and waited too long. Within hours of returning, the bickering began again. All my brave soldiers who had risen to the moment of crisis had gone AWOL.

Life was just as it had been before I left—a little crazy, but still very good.

There's no place like home, Lord.

No place like home.

. . .

Why does it take a crisis to turn me toward You?
Let me see Your hand in the "everyday crises" of life.
You can handle all my crises, big and small.
I'm grateful You made me wait
and taught me to trust again.

And the LORD said unto him,
Who hath made man's mouth?
or who maketh the dumb, or deaf,
or the seeing, or the blind?
have not I the LORD?
EXODUS 4:11

Although I had believed Deborah would be born with Down syndrome,

in the early hours after her birth I hoped I was wrong.

Her doctor's initial assessment was good—he thought she looked normal and responded appropriately. With this encouragement, when I saw her four hours after birth, I began thinking she really was "normal."

Her ears didn't appear as misshapen as at birth; her eyes, which were less puffy, did not look very slanted and did not have the characteristic fold in front. Her hands did not have the single crease often found in Down syndrome.

About the only "different" things were her flatter nose, the extra skin on her neck, and a flatter head in back. Other than that, she looked like all my other babies.

Four hours after this, she turned blue. They detected a heart murmur. Another doctor thought there was Down syndrome.

So much for hope.

But then I was back to faith, where I had begun.

It was the better place to be, because my hope had been in Deborah's appearance, but my faith was in God.

And I knew it was God who had sent her, just as she was. God had called her—with her forty-seven chromosomes—into being in my womb. I knew He would show Himself mighty on her behalf, which He did in Okinawa many times over.

However, despite the early surge of faith, I've had a few lapses. As I've read articles about the condition, I've wondered if I could have done something to prevent it, something to save Deborah the life of trials that awaits her. This is a dangerous thought process, because it is depressing and self-centered; it denies God's hand in my life.

All children—the deaf, the blind, the normal, the abnormal—are His creation. He calls a specific egg and sperm together to make the child He desires. I am but a steward of the little people He creates within me.

It is my job to train them for Him regardless of their health or abilities. Even if He takes them from me before birth (as He has done four times), I must remain faithful to my calling as His instrument of life, knowing that all are sent for His glory.

Deborah was sent—just as she is—for His glory.

Therein rests my faith and hope.

Father, please forgive my faithlessness.
I know You made this child—
with her extra chromosome—
and sent her as a special blessing to us and others.
I'm humbled to have the privilege of
nurturing her in Your love.

A good name is rather to be chosen than great riches,
and loving favour rather than silver and gold.

PROVERBS 22:1

One of the most difficult things about having children is naming them.

I spend hours during each pregnancy thinking through the hundreds of possibilities. I do not want to saddle a child with a moniker he will dislike.

Because I am conservative—I dislike "cute" names, "unisex" names, and those with "alternative" spellings—my list is reasonably short. I also like to use biblical names and names of family members and special friends.

With all these self-imposed restrictions, by the time I got to the eighth child, the name pool was a puddle. So I was very glad that the Lord impressed me with the name "Deborah Helen."

But then a crisis came. When I realized Deborah Helen was not going to be "normal," I did not know if I could give her my name.

I had waited through seven children—including five boys—to name one after me. But this long-awaited one was not going to be perfect. She might not have the brains I so highly valued. And she'd probably look "different."

I didn't know if I could do it, even though I believed God had given the name.

I struggled with this thought several weeks, never mentioning it because I was ashamed. How could I be so vain as to not want any child to have my name? Was I so perfect that I did not want to be identified with an "imperfect" child?

Fortunately, God didn't let me wallow in prideful stupidity too long.

He showed me my brace-needing, thumb-sucking, asthmatic, gifted-but-lazy kids. Not one was perfect.

Nor was I. In fact, nobody was. So what if my baby had forty-seven chromosomes? That was just her imperfection.

If anything, her particular imperfection would require extra effort on her part to succeed. She needed a strong name.

So she was named Deborah Helen for my Internet friend Debbie, who had courageously faced cancer; for her maternal great-grandmother, Helen Kenvin, who practiced assertiveness long before there was a word for it; for her paternal great-grandmother, Helen Fluegel, who was also a determined lady; for another Helen, who is a very godly woman, and, yes, for me.

In her first two weeks, Deborah Helen showed herself strong and determined.

I had to smile.

My "imperfect" child had the perfect name.

Father, I thank You for
this "imperfect" child and her good name.
She fits so well into our imperfect family.
How grateful I am that I can call upon
Your perfect wisdom as I guide her to You.

The Spirit of God hath made me,
and the breath of the Almighty hath given me life.
JOB 33:4

The damage report finally arrived.

We received a "statement of benefits" from our insurance company for Deborah's stay in the Neonatal Intensive Care Unit.

If I had enough money to pay her bill, I'd have enough to buy a new fifteen-passenger van (as priced on Guam, which is several thousand dollars more than in the States).

And of that bill, our insurance company said we owed all of it!

In truth, we will not owe all of it. The claim will be reprocessed when the insurance company receives a form verifying that it is our only insurance company.

It's a stalling tactic. The company is not going to pay anything it is not required to pay. In this day of rampant insurance fraud, I understand that concern. However, it is a little disheartening to have to prove we are entitled to the coverage Mike pays for each month.

It's also a little nerve-wracking. I tend to lose hair color when I'm told I owe a hospital over half of my husband's annual salary.

But while I wait for forms and checks to crisscross the Pacific, I have a chance to think: Just how much is one life worth?

A growing number of people around the world would say that too much has already been spent on Deborah. "It costs the state too much to care for children with Down syndrome," they say. "It's more cost-effective to have amniocentesis and abort them."

An article in the December 2, 1996, issue of *The Weekly Standard* exposed this evil trend.

Thanks to amniocentesis and other prenatal genetic tests, a woman can now learn if she is carrying a baby with Down syndrome. More and more women are choosing to abort those "defective" babies. According to one doctor, in his experience, 90 percent of mothers with a Down syndrome child will choose to terminate their pregnancies (i.e., kill their babies)!

The article also quotes a 1995 study that determined that the total cost for all children born with the disorder in a given year is $1.8 billion. Over a lifetime, each child with Down syndrome will cost society about $451,000. I find such figures dubious, because researchers get creative with definitions. I also find such studies annoying. Where are the studies that show us how much a "normal" person will cost society? Just how much does it cost society to support a normal person who grows up to be a murderer and spends a lifetime in jail?

But let's say the figure is true: $451,000 for a little girl who will give countless smiles, boundless love, and uncritical acceptance, and who will, I believe,

inspire thousands of "normal" people.
That looks like a bargain to me.

. . .

My daughter's life is priceless, Father.
You gave it to her.
I trust that You will make it fruitful.
Let her little life count as much as any life can.
May she serve You to her fullest
and bless many along the way.

Make a joyful noise unto the LORD,
all ye lands.
PSALM 100:1

The baby was crying.

She was hungry, and she was not too happy about having to wait through the rigmarole of getting her situated. It was the morning feeding, when I fed and pumped simultaneously in order to get breast milk for supplementation later in the day.

As I juggled baby, breast, and breast pump, she hollered more.

"I'm coming," I said apologetically, "just hold on."

She cried louder.

"Oh, please, Baby, have patience." I positioned the breast pump.

The cry continued.

The pump bottle slipped.

The cry was now a wail.

Just as I was about to wail myself, I noticed Anna standing near my elbow.

"I love to hear her cry," she said thoughtfully. "It's the most beautiful sound in the world."

I stopped short.

"The most beautiful sound in the world? Why do you think that?"

She smiled sweetly. "Because it is."

I got Deborah to the breast and all was quiet as

she nursed. I thought about Anna's words.

And I had to agree with her.

For some critical hours, we weren't sure that this baby would cry again. Doctors were afraid she had a heart defect. It could have been serious. She could have needed surgery. She could have died.

As she lay there beneath the warmer, wired and tubed, under her oxygen hood, I would have given a million dollars just to hear a whimper, let alone a cry.

I know I'm not alone.

There are women all around the world who long to hold a child, but cannot because they are infertile. Many have had miscarriages. Others have held their precious little ones for a few short hours or days or weeks or months, only to lose them to medical conditions or sudden infant death syndrome. Every one of them would give her life just to hear a baby cry.

When babies cry it means they are here, they are alive. That's cause for celebration, not for annoyance.

When babies cry, they are telling us they have a need only we can meet. When we fill their tummies, change their diapers, and hold them close, we can feel honored. God has chosen us to care for a tiny part of His creation. What an awesome responsibility!

Later in the day when Deborah cried, I didn't pick her up immediately.

I listened for just a moment.

To the most beautiful sound in the world.

A baby's cry is such a joyful noise.
Thank You for her lungs, her voice, her life.
I pray she and all my little ones
will grow to sing Your praises.

Every good gift and every perfect gift is from above,
and cometh down from the Father of lights,
with whom is no variableness,
neither shadow of turning.
JAMES 1:17

I've watched all of my babies carefully,

but I've been watching Deborah very carefully. Every little thing—a coo, a smile, a wide-eyed stare—is noticed, and often cheered.

The night she smiled and cooed for fifteen minutes during church, I was so thrilled I could barely contain myself! The very next day, when she made definite eye contact with her oldest brother, he shouted loud enough to be heard on Saipan: *"She sees me! She sees me!"*

Of course, all of this rejoicing is because of Deborah's syndrome. Since we do not know how much the syndrome will affect her mentally and physically, we are all watching for good signs. Any and every indication—however slight—that she's going to do "better than expected" is cause for celebration.

If we keep this up, when she really starts understanding, she's going to think she's a pretty special child.

And she is. In fact, she is what the state (i.e., the educational system) calls a "special needs" child. This is a euphemistic umbrella term that covers children who have a wide range of mental and physical handicaps (and gives the state a wide door through which to enter private households). I suppose it is nicer than saying a child is "retarded" or "crippled," but the term is misleading.

Certainly, Deborah does have special needs because of her condition, but even "normal" children have special needs.

When my oldest is facing the spiritual battle of his life, he has a special need for my prayers, patience, and support.

The six year old has a special need when she doesn't want to be separated from me, even if it means sitting through a "boring" orchestra concert.

My eight-year-old aircraft designer needs special encouragement, even if I've already seen a thousand Lego airplanes.

Watching my "special needs" baby has reminded me how special all children are. Every new little thing every baby does is miraculous because thousands of cells, impulses, thoughts, and feelings must work together to accomplish it.

I've also been reminded that every child has his own special parent. Each is given to specific parents to fulfill God's wonderful plan in a unique way.

No one else can do the job better; I am already God's best for my children.

Scary thought.

But as I trust in Him, God will enable me to meet the needs of all my special children.

All my children are special gifts to me, and I to them.
Help us all be grateful for each other and for the opportunity
to honor and serve You in our family.
Meet our special needs according to Your great mercy.
We're trusting in You, Lord.

Therefore I say unto you,
Take no thought for your life. . . .
Which of you by taking thought can
add one cubit unto his stature?
MATTHEW 6:25, 27

I have a "Type A" personality.

In practical terms, I'm a perfectionistic, high-strung, workaholic who doesn't know what it means to "rest."

I've tried to control these tendencies. I've bought organizers to help me handle my commitments, but have been too busy to write in them. I've collected chairs to encourage myself to sit down, but never had time to use them.

And I've prayed: "Lord, slow me down."

Over the years, God answered that prayer in unexpected ways. He gave me pregnancies requiring bed rest; a broken leg; a long winter in South Dakota.

Each time, I'd learn about patience and about the joys of taking life slowly, and I'd vow to change. But once the slow time had passed, I'd be running full speed again. And soon I'd be praying, "Lord, please slow me down."

He answered me again. He gave me Deborah.

Thanks to her extra little twenty-first chromosome, little Deborah has slowed me down.

First, she took me away from the usual routine. For two weeks I was alone with her on foreign soil. No family. No phone. No lengthy to-do list. I did little more than eat, feed the baby, and pray.

Then we got home, and she didn't gain weight. For the next month, I sat on one of my underused chairs. I nursed and pumped and rocked and nursed and pumped some more.

Between feedings, we began her therapy:

Massage the cheeks. "Oooo, doesn't that feel good? Oops. Put that tongue in your mouth."

Lift and exercise the legs. "Let's bicycle. One, two, three, four, one, two, three, four. You're gonna have great abs!"

Toes to the mouth. "Eat those toes. Get that mouth moving."

Roll side to side. "Roll the baby left, roll the baby right. Bring that head over—that's it."

Flip onto tummy. Arms underneath chest, support shoulders and—"C'mon, Honey, pick up your head—that's it! Good!"

It's repetitious, methodical, slow.

And it is wondrously rewarding. Unlike her siblings, who raced through their early milestones, Deborah is working through hers. And because I'm helping her work, I get to see each skill develop.

Slowly, Deborah is teaching me that growth and life are miracles that should not be taken for granted, or wasted in frenzied pursuits.

And I'm learning.

Slowly.

I have cared so much for
the worthless accomplishments of life, Father.
I've spent much of my time hurrying
toward goals that have little value.
Thank You for giving me a goal that is
worth achieving, a life worth developing.
Let me have the patience to do it
according to Your timing, slowly.

For the LORD seeth not as man seeth;
for man looketh on the outward appearance,
but the LORD looketh on the heart.

1 SAMUEL 16:7

When Deborah was born,
she looked "normal" to many people.

At first, my Chamorro obstetrician and Chinese pediatrician said she looked fine. Her eyes looked different to me. And her ears were small and misshapen.

Within a day, Caucasian doctors said she did have enough features of the syndrome to warrant genetic testing.

Soon her condition was obvious to me. But as the days in Okinawa passed and I kept staring at my baby, her appearance changed. One day, I realized her ears were quite normal. Though small, they were perfectly shaped. When asleep, she looked like every other baby from the Middlebrooke Baby Factory.

Toward the end of our time in the Neonatal ICU, I was staring at Deborah when a nurse came by. She looked at us thoughtfully.

"I don't know what it is," I told her, "but she looks more normal to me now. I don't know if she's actually changed, or if I'm just getting used to the difference."

The nurse nodded and smiled a knowing-nurse smile. "You're getting used to it."

In my heart I knew it was not just conditioning.

To my eyes, she really didn't look that "Down-sy."

Now eight months old, she looks just like the rest of us.

Her eyes are big and round, like all her siblings'. They slant ever so slightly. They look normal until she cries. But then, all babies' eyes look normal until they cry.

Her ears are perfectly shaped, but small, just like those of one brother.

She sticks out her tongue frequently. But so do two of her very normal siblings.

She's not sitting up yet, but another one didn't sit well until his first birthday.

Am I denying her condition? No. I see it in her, especially from the side, because then the flatness of her face is more apparent. But I also see that she looks a little like all of us, which is how God wanted her to look.

One morning, Thomas was staring at her thoughtfully.

"Mom, didn't you say Deborah was born with Down syndrome?"

"Yes, she was."

"And didn't you say people with Down syndrome look different?"

"When they grow up, they may."

"But she doesn't look at all different."

Not to a brother's eyes.

Not to eyes of love.

*Thank You for the eyes of a child
who looks with a heart full of love.
Let me always see my special child as You see her,
knowing she is perfect in Your eyes.*

Now unto him that is able to do exceeding
abundantly above all that we ask or think,
according to the power that worketh in us,
Unto him be glory in the church
by Christ Jesus throughout all ages,
world without end. Amen.
EPHESIANS 3:20–21

"Above all that we ask or think."

An auditorium filled to overflowing on Sundays.

Ten thousand people saved in one crusade.

A million-dollar ministry that depends on faith.

"Above all that we ask or think."

George Mueller sitting at a table surrounded by hungry orphans, praying for food. In minutes, supper arrives at the door in the hands of a stranger.

Corrie Ten Boom walking out of a German prison camp.

Elisabeth Elliot, with her small daughter in hand, going into the jungle of Ecuador to live with the Auca Indians, the very people who murdered her husband and four other missionaries.

"Above all that we ask or think."

A free car.

A job promotion.

A seven-figure income.

"Above all that we ask or think."

Why does this come to mind when a person

receives a material blessing or has his circumstances altered miraculously?

Is "exceeding abundance" only seen and touched? I think not.

A little girl with Down syndrome was beyond anything I would ask for. I thought I did not have the temperament, the time, the skill, or the heart for a special child.

But God sent her anyway.

In so doing, He did an exceedingly abundant work. He took me through a dark valley after her birth, showing me the frailty of her life. Then He filled my heart with love and joy and hope for all this child will be, all this child will do.

He has shown me that He will protect her. She is His. He has shared her with me for reasons that are beyond what I can yet imagine.

Because of His work within, when I look at her, I am not discouraged. I see the miracle she is. And I am humbled that He would give her to me.

The greatest miracles are beyond what we can see.

They are found in the exceeding abundance of His love within our hearts.

You have done a great work within my heart, Father,
and I am grateful.
I pray Your Spirit will do far greater works
within and without in the days ahead.

Inspirational Library

Beautiful purse/pocket-size editions of Christian classics bound in flexible leatherette. These books make thoughtful gifts for everyone on your list, including yourself!

When I'm on My Knees   The highly popular collection of devotional thoughts on prayer, especially for women.
Flexible Leatherette $4.97

The Bible Promise Book   Over 1,000 promises from God's Word arranged by topic. What does God promise about matters like: Anger, Illness, Jealousy, Love, Money, Old Age, and Mercy? Find out in this book!
Flexible Leatherette $3.97

Daily Wisdom for Women   A daily devotional for women seeking biblical wisdom to apply to their lives. Scripture taken from the New American Standard Version of the Bible.
Flexible Leatherette $4.97

My Daily Prayer Journal   Each page is dated and features a Scripture verse and ample room for you to record your thoughts, prayers, and praises. One page for each day of the year.
Flexible Leatherette $4.97

Available wherever books are sold.
Or order from:

Barbour Publishing, Inc.
P.O. Box 719
Uhrichsville, OH 44683
http://www.barbourbooks.com

If you order by mail, add $2.00 to your order for shipping.
Prices are subject to change without notice.